Séance 101

Physical Mediumship:

Table Tipping, Psychic Photography, Trumpet Séances,
and Other Important Phenomena

Schiffer Publishing Ltd®

4880 Lower Valley Road   Atglen, Pennsylvania   19310

Published by Schiffer Publishing Ltd.
4880 Lower Valley Road
Atglen, PA 19310
Phone: (610) 593-1777; Fax: (610) 593-2002
E-mail: Info@schifferbooks.com

For the largest selection of fine reference books on this and related subjects, please visit our web site at
www.schifferbooks.com
We are always looking for people to write books on new and related subjects. If you have an idea for a book
please contact us at the above address.

This book may be purchased from the publisher.
Include $3.95 for shipping.
Please try your bookstore first.
You may write for a free catalog.

In Europe, Schiffer books are distributed by
Bushwood Books
6 Marksbury Ave.
Kew Gardens
Surrey TW9 4JF England
Phone: 44 (0) 20 8392-8585; Fax: 44 (0) 20 8392-9876
E-mail: info@bushwoodbooks.co.uk
Website: www.bushwoodbooks.co.uk
Free postage in the U.K., Europe; air mail at cost.

Other Schiffer Books by Elaine M. Kuzmeskus
Connecticut Ghosts

Copyright © 2007 by Elaine Kuzmeskus
Library of Congress Control Number: 2007927044

Designed by Mark David Bowyer
Type set in ProseAntique / New Baskerville BT

ISBN: 978-0-7643-2717-9
Printed in China

Contents

From the time I was in my crib I have seen spirit guides. First a Hindu guru, then a tall, handsome Egyptian, and later spirit doctor, Dr. Lang, along with guidance from Jack Kerouac and Reverend Arthur Ford. Upon request, Arthur Ford's name materialized with a tiny red heart beside it on my spirit card. Spirit indeed lives!

History of mediumship from the seers of Ancient Egypt and Greece to the Old Testament prophets, Moses, and Elias reviewed. Why do Spiritualists view Jesus as a master medium? What knowledge do the Tibetan masters and South American shamans share about the super-physical world?

Modern mediumship began when the Fox sisters heard rappings from a deceased peddler. Soon the movement spread throughout the United States and England. By the turn of the century, two major Spiritualist camps were established Lily Dale Assembly in New York and Camp Chesterfield in Indiana.

The United States and England have produced some of the finest physical mediums. Discover the extraordinary physical mediumship of the Fox sisters, D. D. Home, the Bangs sisters, Margery Crandon, Helen Duncan, and Leslie Flint. While D. D. Home demonstrated levitation, Edgar Cayce established medical clairvoyance. Great literature, art, and music have also been channeled by spirit.

What is esoteric anatomy? How do charkas and nadis govern inner development? What are the mechanics of physical mediumship, ecto-plasm, and akasha? Table tipping is the first step to developing physical mediumship as it helps to boost the the vibrations needed for contact with spirit. Learn the basics of table tipping from the New England School of Metaphysics.

When the photographer is in rapport, spirits will readily manifest on film. William Mumler, Billy Hope, and professional ghost hunter Troy Taylor have given us many fine examples of psychic photography. Learn how the orb photos used in *Connecticut Ghosts* were obtained with both standard and digital cameras.

Ghost-hunters and paranormal researchers use Electronic Voice Phe-nomena as a tool to contact spirits. An examination of early work done in electronic voice phenomena by Konstatine Raudive, George Meek, and today's EVP researchers, Lisa and Tom Butler. The dead definitely talk!

Learn how to safely open the third eye with Tibetan and Spiritualist techniques. At first, spirit lights, and colors are seen—later, the outline of spirit and finally the full figure. Some spirit artists, like Coral Polge in England and Reverend Rita Berkowtiz in the United States, can even draw their guides!

After mediums have gained rapport with their guides through clair-voyance, they are ready to deepen trance with meditation, breathing, and hypnosis. Next, Spiritualist instructions on how to set up a séance room. What seating arrangement, sounds, smells, and attitudes draw in guides, loved ones, and angels?

Spirit communication is often filled with sound psychology, philosophy, and science. Helen Schulman, Jane Roberts, Elwood Babbitt, along with today's trance channelers, Gordon Michael Scallion, Glenda Green, and Ronna Hermann, are some of the finest trance mediums. What messages did Seth, the Tibetan, Vishnu, Mother Mary, Jesus, and the angels have for humanity? Do we truly create our own reality? Is the world on the verge of a spiritual break-through? What is our collective future?

     Trance diagnosticians Andrew Jackson Davis, Edgar Cayce, and psychic surgeons Jose Arigo and Alex Orbito have helped millions obtain health. When premiere channeler, Elwood Babbitt, autographed his book, *Perfect Health* with "Accept no substitutes," he meant it!

     An overview of this rare but real aspect of physical mediumship. Not only can spirit messages be amplified through the trumpet, but apports can be transported as well! Trumpet mediumship both here and abroad examined. The chapter concludes with advice on development from famed trumpet medium, Reverend Suzanne Greer. Learn how a "cabinet" is used and the importance of a "gate-keeper."

     What is this rare form of mediumship in which spirit materialized picture on canvas, cards, and silk? Only a few mediums—the Bangs sisters and the Campbell brothers, as well as Reverend Hoyt Robinette possess this amazing ability. During his sessions, Reverend Robinette places blank index cards and colored pens with their caps still on into a covered basket. The spirits are able to create phenomenal drawings, photos, portraits, and names on the cards while the covered basket remains in plain sight!

     First trance, then transfiguration, and finally full materialization of spirit is possible. This is a very rare and much-faked form of mediumship. What distinguishes the real materializations of mediums, such as Helen Duncan, from the cheats who make their way to Spiritualist camps? How does the "psychic mafia" defraud the public? Sitter beware!

     What is magic? What is magical mediumship? Margery Crandon was the last of the great physical mediums. In 1924, Houdini was infuriated when he heard that the *Scientific American* was about to award Margery the prize of $2,500 for her extraordinary mediumship. What happened in the séance room when Harry Houdini investigated Boston's Medium Margery made national headlines. Finally, what message did the spirit of Harry Houdini bring through Spiritualist medium, Reverend Arthur Ford?

Dedication

This book is lovingly dedicated to Reverend Kenneth and Reverend Gladys Custance.

Each was "the teacher who walks in the shadow of the temple, among his followers, lives not of his wisdom but rather of his faith and lovingness."

—Kahlil Gibran

Acknowledgments

First and foremost, I would like to acknowledge Dr. Susan Roberts, who edited the first draft. It is always a pleasure to work with a friend. I would also like to acknowledge Reverend Hoyt Robinette, Reverend Gail Hicks, Reverend Suzanne Greer, and Reverend Patricia Kennedy who introduced me to the world of physical mediumship. Also, I would like to thank the staff at Camp Chesterfield in Indiana, the staff at the Theosophical Society in America in Illinois, and the staff at Lily Dale Assembly in New York for their support. Finally, I would like to extend thanks to Schiffer Publishing, in particular Peter Schiffer and Dinah Roseberry; and to Jeff Snyder for his assistance with my first effort—*Connecticut Ghosts*.

Introduction:
Spirit Lives!

"If our personality survives then it is strictly logical or scientific to assume that it retains memory, intellect, other faculties, and knowledge that we require on this earth. Therefore if personality exists after what we call death, it is reasonable to conclude that those who left the earth would like to communicate with those they have left here."

—Thomas Edison

Have you ever casually snapped a photograph, only to see several "extras" in the developed picture? Perhaps you have played a tape back to find the voice of Grandpa who died many moons ago. Sometimes spirit will actually materialize before your eyes. It is even possible to travel astrally from one continent to the another. I know—as a Spiritualist medium—for I have experienced all of these things.

Was I frightened by physical mediumship? No, as ever since I can recall, I have been able to close my eyes and see a guide present. At first it was a slightly built, bare-chested Hindu clothed in a white muslin dhoti and matching turban. Later, it was a handsome Egyptian master wearing a striped headdress with a cobra rising from the middle of his forehead—a spot I would later call the third eye. Just looking into his magnetic brown eyes would make my head swirl, so intense was the master's gaze. Later, as I began to do readings for others, an ancient Chinese doctor came in to assist. Clairvoyantly, I could see the blacked-robed physician with a black pill-box hat take the pulse of a client or examine the unsuspecting pulse of a sitter.

While the Hindu, Egyptian, and Chinese masters did not give their names, other guides did—notably Dr. Lang. For several months, I heard the name "Dr Lang" pop up clairaudiently as I did readings for clients. When I inquired of the spirit, "Who are you?" Dr. Lang explained patiently that he too had been interested in parapsychology. After some research, I found that a Dr. Andrew Lang had indeed been an early turn of the century researcher in parapsychology.

Angels have also made their appearance. They remain lovingly detached when they offer suggestions. This was certainly the case when I awoke early one day with severe stomach pains. What to do? Should I wake up my husband, Ron, and head for the emergency room or wait it out? When I went to my office to meditate, an angel sat down beside me and with great love, gently assured me, "Every effort will be made to keep you in the body." I decided no more emergency medical assistance was necessary. The advice was sound, as the stomach pains turned out to be a twenty-four hour bug.

Spirit doctors, by the way, do not hesitate to give specific advice—just the opposite of angels. I know. Once, when I was suffering a bout of bronchitis, a spirit doctor, firmly said, "An expectorant is needed." Not familiar with the term "expectorate," I perused the labels of over-counter medications at our local pharmacy until the word appeared in the label.

Sure enough, the cough syrup with "expectorate" eased my chest pain. While many guides have come in over the years, the guidance from my first master has proven extremely accurate. The spirit of a Hindu swami greeted me when I was in my crib. Later, at about four, he began to monitor and correct errors in my thoughts. About this time my family was living in an apartment house in Los Angeles, California. Our next door neighbor, an elderly lady, loved children and often would invite my younger sister, Barbara, and me across the hall for a visit. On one such visit, I looked over her shoulder and saw her son, a Korean vet, bandaging the stump of recently amputated leg. Quickly, I turned away. My Hindu guide telepathically told me, "Don't turn away. Someday you may marry a man who has lost his leg." I then felt a rush of compassion for the veteran.

Later I learned just how accurate the advice was. My future husband, Ronald Kuzmeskus, was seven at the time. When he was fourteen, he developed severe blood poisoning. The doctors told his parents it would be necessary to amputate the infected leg in order to save him. His father, Anthony Kuzmeskus, a practical father, thought for bit and said, "No, I don't want a son without a leg." Maybe he was just stubborn or a little bit psychic. Many years later, I was to record the voice of my father-in-law, now deceased, on tape saying "Protect Anthony." I guess he is still protecting Ron, who by the way, did make it though the night and fully recovered without any surgery. However, at the time, my Hindu guide had made the prophecy, the possibility of marrying a man with amputated limb was a definite possibility.

When I was five, my Hindu guide, a slight man in his forties with a white cotton turban and white dhoti, began to instruct me on meditation. "Cross your index fingers and place then over your third eyes and press gently." Soon, I was seeing bright colors and lights with my eyes closed. Later I was to learn that crossing the fingers or hands in a mudra balances the right hemisphere of the brain. I once described this experience to Dr. Douglas Baker, an MD who is clairvoyant. He assured me it was a safe practice as long as I didn't press too hard. "Placing your crossed finger over your third eye stimulates the optic nerve hence the clairvoyance."

About the same time, I was instructed in remote viewing. When I was worried about my mother, I asked my Hindu guide, "Will she ever improve?"

"Just visualize your mother in your mind's eye and keep pushing her forward into the future and you can see for yourself."

Sadly, as I looked into the future, I saw little change. Apparently, it would be many years before there would be a change for the better. A few years later, in 1955, my parents separated and my mother's drinking increased. It wasn't until the 1980s, when Momma almost died from a heart attack, that she stopped drinking for good. This early venture into remote viewing left me with no desire to continue the practice as a child.

However, my clairvoyant adventures continued. I took them as natural occurrence, and believed everyone was psychic. By the time I was in the third grade, I realized this was not true. Still, I could not deny my reality. For example, my third grade teacher, Mrs. McGinty, had the students observe a drop of pink hand lotion under a microscope. When it came my turn, I eagerly peered in the lens of the microscope and saw pink bubbles, I also heard a male voice say: "That's your birthday present." This didn't make sense to me, as my birthday had been the day before and I wasn't expecting any more presents. I just "knew" intuitively the present would not be the microscope or the lotion, but the pink bubbles which made no sense.

Usually, I would just let such thought go, but this one stayed with me the rest of the day in school. When I came home, my grandmother greeted me at the door with a pink box embossed with bubbles.

"This is your birthday present," Nana said cheerfully. "Aunt Polly and Uncle John could not make your party yesterday, so they dropped their gift off."

I think there was a bracelet inside, but I am not quite sure; however, I will never forget the pink bubbles embossed on the box or the uncanny message!

Two years later my grandmother died. For many months, I would rush home after school expecting Nana to greet me at the door. Sadly, her physical presence was no longer with us. However, I would often feel her spirit present as I grew more inward. Later, though, as I became a shy teenager, my clairvoyance seemed to diminish.

When I was eighteen, my Hindu guide again came in loud and clear. For example, once when I was just getting out of the shower, I saw two twelve-inch squares; one emerald green and the other royal blue. I closed my eyes in disbelief, but when I opened them, they were still there. It was the Hindu guide again. He came in even stronger in my dreams and began giving me instructions: "Sound can be seen and color can be heard." He began to lecture on vibration and explained the energy systems about the third eye, throat, and heart that could be increased in intensity by placing a stone there.

It wasn't long before my Hindu guide was instructing me in astral travel. One afternoon during my regular meditation session, I experienced astral travel. After the initial few breaths, I felt my spirit leave through my third eye and float through the ceiling very quickly. Within minutes, I had bilocated to India and landed in a beautiful pool of turquoise water. I looked up and my Hindu guide was there to instruct me. Telepathically, he indicated that I should look at a newspaper about twenty feet away. Sensing the newspaper had an important message for me, I tried in vain to pull myself over the edge of the pool. The white-turbaned swami only shook his head and pointed to the three stairs at the edge of the pool. With considerably more grace, I took the three steps out of the pool, but was still too far from the newspaper to read it. Again, I looked to my guide for direction. "Draw it near with your third eye," he advised. Concentrating on my third eye, the Sunday Edition of the *Boston Globe* was beneath my eyes, with the prophetic date, April 23. Three years later, on April 23, 1972, I conducted my first Spiritualist church service—the final test to become a Spiritualist medium!

Since then, other guides have come in to be identified in dreams. That is how I met the writer, Jack Kerouac, who encouraged me in my writing, stating, "Fame is on your horizon." In a vivid dream, I saw a handsome man in the stripped robes of an Essene—I immediately sensed we had known each other as Essenes. (Essenes were the mystical Jewish sect which included Jesus and his family.) Then he gave his name as "Jack Kerouac" and said he had been interested in the work of Edgar Cayce and the Essenes, as well as many spiritual matters. Since there was no way to verified the information, I just shrugged it off.

Later, in 1981, I was attracted to a library book, *Off the Road: My Years with Cassady, Kerouac, and Ginsberg* by Carolyn Cassady. I checked the memoir out. Sure enough, all that the spirit of Jack Kerouac had told me was true: "In 1956, an event took place that surprised and delighted us [Carolyn and Neal Cassady] a book named, *The Search for Bridey Murphy* was published, and it caused a furor because it supported the evidence for reincarnation. To us it was perplexing that this book should receive so much a attention, rather than a book such as *Many Mansions* written by modern scientists. Through our reading on the subject, we had discovered extensive literature from every century which was already available but ignored by the standard-setters of the day." Her husband, best friend of Jack Kerouac, "jumped for joy" because he believed in this book that Cayce was correct in his belief in reincarnation. Both Carolyn and Neal went on to attend sessions with Hugh Lynn Cayce and Elsie Sechrist, as well as have a past-life reading with Dr. Hunter.

According to Carolyn, they shared their studies of Edgar Cayce and reincarnation with Jack Kerouac. In fact, Jack Kerouac was very "up" on Edgar Cayce, and theories of reincarnation and karma as well as in Buddhism. Once he remarked to Carolyn that he believed he felt his chronic phlebitis was the result of his cruelties as a football player in his youth. After reading *Off the Road*, I realized that my communication with Jack Kerouac was authentic. Every now and then my writing goes very well—seven or eight pages without missing a beat. I am reminded of Kerouac's habit of taping sheets of paper together, not wishing to stop to insert new paper. When this crazy flow of writing starts, I "know" I am being guided by the hands of a much more experienced writer. On these rare occasions, I say softly under my breath, "Thank you, Jack!"

Arthur Ford made contact with me when I was asked to do the Houdini Séance. I was just about to decline the invitation, when I heard a male voice say, "Houdini has a message for you." That was my introduction to Reverend Arthur Ford. Since then he has guided me to the Lily Dale Assembly and to the Arthur Findlay College in England, as he has impressed upon me that it was time to deepen my trance. When I began to do some research on Arthur Ford, I learned some unsettling information. While most of his publicity was positive, toward the end of his career some of his incredible mediumship came into question. Alan Vaugh claimed that Ford was "cheating" because he found newspaper clippings of many deceased people in his files. When I telepathically questioned Arthur Ford, his spirit replied: "I was doing my homework—trying to gain rapport with the deceased before the actual séance." I can relate to his response as I did the same thing before I did the Houdini Séance. I read Doug Henning's book, *Houdini: His Legend and His Magic*, to make contact with the master magician before the séance—which I did. Two days before the Halloween séance, I sent the thought out: "Houdini, if you plan to be at the séance, I need to see you." Within minutes, to my astonished eyes, the spirit of the great magician dressed in an elegant 1920 tuxedo appeared in the doorway of my bedroom. I should not have been so surprised. After all, Houdini was a great performer who understood the need for a dress rehearsal.

When I was doing research for another project, *Connecticut Ghosts*, I switched gears and focused on physical phenomena—psychic photography and electromagnetic energy. Using standard digital and movie camera equipment, I was able to capture some of the spirits on film. Apparently, places like Hill Stead Museum and the Mark Twain House still have spiritual hosts. Just seeing the spirits of Mark Twain's daughter Susie, sitting between her mother and their maid, gave me goose bumps. Susie died in that house. The three female spirits were most graciously greeting me from the round settee in the spacious entry hall of the Mark Twain home. Their smiling faces seemed to give approval to the book. Physical mediumship also played a central role in *Connecticut Ghosts*. Ever since I conducted the Houdini Séance in 1997, I have had a fascination with physical phenomena. Is it the influence of Houdini or Reverend Arthur Ford? I think not. Houdini loudly condemned Spiritualists—even testifying before Congress to ban mediumship.

Reverend Arthur Ford was known for his spectacular platform work in which he gave both the first and last names of spirit through clairaudince. While he was not technically known for physical mediumship, he was a very gifted trance mediumship. While in trance, his guide, Fletcher, took control of Reverend Ford's faculties and Fletcher became the go between, When Fletcher acted as the medium, Ford had no conscious recall of the sessions.

While Reverend Ford has certainly encouraged my work in physical phenomena, I believe there is another medium assisting from the other side—Boston medium Margery Crandon. I was introduced to her phenomenal physical mediumship when I did research for the Houdini Séance. Margery Crandon was a trumpet medium, a feat which even today is quite rare. While in a deep trance, she was able to raise a light megaphone, or trumpet, through which spirits could speak their messages. Not only was Margery Crandon the most famous medium of the 1920s, but she also was the most researched.

Professors from Harvard and the Boston and New York Societies for Psychical Research thoroughly tested and validated her trumpet mediumship. News of her extraordinary physical mediumship spread to England. Arthur Findlay came over from England to investigate her. After several sittings with the trumpet medium, he pronounced Margery Crandon "the eighth wonder of the world." Margery Crandon died in 1941, before I was born, so I was never able to see her physical mediumship in person. While some may even scoff at the idea for trance, psychic photography, and trumpet mediumship, I can assure you it is a genuine, though a rare gift of the spirit. I have had the privilege of witnessing sessions of physical mediumship of premiere trance channeler Elwood Babbitt with whom I had annual readings, from 1980 until a year before his death in 2000. It was such a thrill to see Elwood go into a deep trance, and within minutes, the erudite voice of Dr. Fisher would come through the sleeping farmer-medium dressed in jeans and a flannel plaid shirt he favored.

Occasionally, I would forget and address the entranced medium as "Elwood." An indignant but polite voice would insist; "This is Doctor Fisher speaking." Elwood Babbitt as well as other illustrious guides included Mark Twain, Albert Einstein, Mathatma Ghandi, Jesus Christ, and the Vishnu. In addition to mediumship, Elwood channeled many books, including *Talks with Christ* and *The God Within: Testament of the Vishnu* and *Perfect Health: Accept No Substitute*.

Shortly after Elwood Babbitt passed over, I met another trance medium, Reverend Hoyt Robinette. His gifts of the spirit include manifestation of spirit pictures and names on cards and silk, as well as trumpet mediumship and billet séances. (In a billet séance, the blind-folded medium answers questions addressed to spirit written on cards or billets. See glossary.)

While Reverend Hoyt Robinette does a spectacular billet séance, he is best known for his spirit card séances. When in trance, Dr. Kenner, Reverend Robinette's control takes over the séance in which spirits actually draw pictures on ordinary three-by-five index cards. The spirits not only draw portraits of guides, but the names of guides and loved ones appear on the back of the cards! I have attended several of his séances in Connecticut, Massachusetts, Maryland, and Indiana. At these séances, I've received pictures of guides, including Dr. Cathcart and Dr. Rinehart, my spirit doctor guides. Before the third spirit card séance, I telepathically said to the spirit of Arthur Ford, "If you are my guide, please sign my card." No one else, including Hoyt, knew of this request. Sure enough, when I examined the names of the back of the card, there was a small red heart followed by the name, Arthur Ford, neatly printed in green letters (page 144). No one can give a greater demonstration of physical mediumship than Reverend Hoyt Robinette!

Camp Chesterfield, in Indiana where Reverend Robinette received his training, proudly proclaims in bold letters over the altar: "Spirit Lives." After reading about the table tipping, psychic photography, trumpet séances, and other aspects of physical mediumship, I hope you will share the same enthusiastic belief—spirit does indeed live!

Jack Kerouac (1922-1969).
Author of *On the Road*.

Reverend Arthur Ford (1897-1971), Spiritualist Minister.

Chapter One:
Roots of Mediumship

"The greatest discovery of any generation is that a human being can alter his life by altering his attitude."

—William James

Mediumship has it roots in ancient times. Seers were plentiful in ancient Egypt. Later, the Greeks raised mediumship to new glamour, erecting great temples to house their channelers who were revered much like today's film stars. The Greeks, in turn, tutored the Romans in the art of divination. Augurs, channelers, and astrologers were routinely consulted by those in power. The desire to know the future was not confined to the pagan population, for Jews and early Christians also dabbled in the occult. Both the Old and New testaments of the *Bible* abound in references to dreams, prophets, and mediums. Old Testament prophets such as Abraham, Jeremiah, and Ezekiel commanded much respect. In the New Testament, the birth of Christ is foretold by astrologers, the three Wise Men. Later Joseph was warned in a dream to return home by a another route lest Herod take the life of baby Jesus. As Jesus faced persecution, the spirits of Moses and Elijah appeared to Jesus. Spiritualists view the transfiguration as an excellent example of a séance with full materialization. Revelations, the last book of the *Bible*, Chapter I, verse 10 and Chapter 4, verse 1, both make references the use of trumpets. Could this be related trumpet mediumship?

No where in human history was mediumship given more respect than in ancient Egypt. Here, thousands of years before Christ, the art of communicating between the two worlds was perfected. Knowledge of the after life was both common and sacred. Priests and priestesses routinely went into hypnotic trance to commune with gods, such as the great god, Sekhmet.[1] *The Egyptian Book of the Dead* reflects a preoccupation with the world beyond. In fact, respect for trance-induced visions was so great that when the Pharaoh Akhnaton saw a transcendental vision of the one God, he changed. He threw out all the old gods in order to worship the "one true god." Later, he and his wife, Neferititi, were forced out of power because of this drastic change.[2]

China also has had a strong mystical tradition. In the first century A.D., Wang Ch'ung chronicled the trance channeling called "wu," a practice commonly accepted in China: "Among men the dead speak through living persons whom they throw into a trance, and the wu thrumming black chords call down the souls of the dead who speak through the mouth of the wu."[3] Much of China's Taoist literature abounds with mystical philosophy. For example, during trying circumstances, one is reminded "what of all things most yielding (water) can overwhelm that which is of all things most hard (rock)." Could these verses have been channeled metaphors? It is well known in astrology that water represents intuition, hence it is the faculty of intuition that can overwhelm rock or the earth. The Chinese see intuition as the strongest protector on the earth.

Tibet, now part of China, also has a long tradition of mysticism. Of the Buddhist countries, it is considered the most spiritual. As each Dali Lama passes into spirit, an oracle is consulted and a group of monks is dispatched to find the new incarnation of the deceased Dali Lama. Death is depicted as a sacred journey in *The Tibetan Book of the Dead.* This classic text on death and dying teaches that the soul goes through a series of planes or bardos. Then, the soul looks into a Mirror of Karma, a process similar to the weighing of the heart described in *Egyptian Book of the Dead.* Tibetan monks are trained to communicate with the spirits of the dead in order to aid the soul in its transition from this world to the next. First-year monks read *The Tibetan Book of Mental Development,* a classic text on the development of mental and mystical powers.

Many find the wisdom of the ages in the Hindu classics, the *Vedas*. Some believe that *Vedas* were received in channeled form by the rishis some 5,000 years ago. Whatever their source, the *Vedas* are filled with knowledge—astrology, ayurvedic medicine, and meditation—that indicates a remarkable understanding of human consciousness. According to the *Vedas*, all thought and feeling are recoded in the akasha. Could it be the ancient rishis have possessed the ability to read these askashic records?

The Greeks also believed in a life after death and referred to heaven as the Eleusian Fields. Greek philosophers such as Pythagoras and Plato were initiated into the Eleusian mystery schools which were said to have originated in ancient Egypt. These cults taught the wisdom of the Egyptian sage Hermes Trismegistus based on the sage's belief in resurrection of the spirit after death.[4] The Greeks believed the god, Aesculapius, was responsible for healing, and they dedicated many temples to him. With their superior knowledge of trance, they developed superior mediums, called Pythias, who were possessed by the gods and then prophesized. Clients of the Pythia included Alexander the Great who was told, "My son thou art invincible." He went on to conquer much of the ancient world.

According to noted author and researcher Dr. Jeffrey Mishlove, the first recorded controlled parapsychological experiment was conducted Greece in the sixth century B.C. Croesus, King of Lydia, sent his messengers out to test the oracles of Aba, Miletus, Dodona, Delphi, Amphiarus, Trophonius, and Jupiter Ammon. They were told to ask the oracles on the appointed day, what the king was doing. At the time of the query, the king had decided to cook a meal of lamb and tortoise. However, before the messenger had a chance to ask, the oracle of Delphi replied, "My senses perceive an odor as one cooks together the flesh of the tortoise and the lamb!"[6]

Later, scholars believe Pythagorus was influenced by the mystery cult of Orpheus. His disciples were said to go through a five-year period of strict silence before being permitted to talk to Pythagorus. The master was also said to possess memories of all his past lives in addition to having heard the harmony of the spheres during inner contemplation.[7] Socrates also credited much of his wisdom to his guide or daemon: "By favor of the Gods, I have since my childhood been attended by a semi-divine being whose voice form time to time dissuades me form some undertaking, but never directs me what I am to do." His student, Plato, continued the philosophy of Socrates' teaching that the soul passes through death and incarnates again, forgetting its past lives.

Romans also used divination to their advantage. Cicero (106 B.C.- 43 B.C.), Rome's most acclaimed orator, even wrote a book, *Divination*, in which he implies that some events are indeed fated, others can be changed with free will. Seneca, a stoic, believed that self development was a means to developing higher consciousness. Galen, one of the founders of modern medicine, used dreams to diagnose and cure illness. In fact, divination was held in such high esteem, that in 150 A.D., the Romans made a law that no important decision could be made without consulting the augurs![8]

From the time of Moses to the ministry of Jesus, the *Bible* also abounds references to the occult which including mediumship, for mediumship was a common practice, as was the belief in reincarnation. For example, Saul requested the services of a medium when frustrated that God had not answered his questions in dreams or prophecy: "Then Saul said unto his servants, 'Seek me a woman who hath familiar spirit that I may go and enquire of her.' And his servant said to him, 'Behold there is a woman that hath a familiar spirit at Endor.'" (I Samuel 28:7) When Saul visited the medium at Endor, the spirit of Samuel was successfully summoned.

Perhaps the most fascinating account of mediumship is found in the New Testament's account known as "the Transfiguration." Here the spirits of Moses and Elijah communicated with Jesus. In Spiritualism, transfiguration of spirit is an aspect of mediumship. Not surprisingly, Jesus demonstrated complete mastery over the earth: levitation when he walked on water, alchemy when he turned the water into wine at Cana, and materialization when he fed the multitude fish and bread.

The *Bible* also alludes to the universal acceptance of reincarnation at the time of Jesus. For example, Jesus was asked if he was " Elijah come again." He signified that he was not an incarnation of the prophet Elijah, but rather the recently beheaded John the Baptist was Elijah, with the reply: "Elijah was here and you knew him not." Of course, the greatest miracle of Jesus was that of the ascension. After his crucifixion, Jesus is sometimes reported as being non-physical (1 Peter 3:18 RSV) but also physical (Luke 24:39). Jesus instructed Mary, " Do not touch me." (John, 20:17) Why? Could it be that his ascended body was so filled with light that it could be harmful to Mary?

Few Christians realize the full significance of ascension, which means to literally take the physical body with you at death. Elizabeth Clare Prophet states that, "Ascended masters are enlightened spiritual beings who once lived on earth just like we do. Over the course of many lifetimes of devotion and striving, they fulfilled their mission and reason for being—their divine plan—and ascended back to their divine source, reuniting with Spirit."[9] Edgar Cayce's guides also speak of the spiritual mastery of Jesus. According to Cayce's source, Jesus was Adam, the first man who, through many lives, overcame the earth. Both Edgar Cayce and Elizabeth Clare Prophet would concur that Jesus set the pattern for humanity.

The *Bible* is filled with references to mystical processes such as ascension. For example, one which stands out in every Sunday-schooler's mind is Daniel's handwriting on the wall (Daniel 8:1). Spiritualists view this as an example of independent/automatic writing.

When Moses mentioned the Ark of Covenant, a device through which the voice of God spoke to the chosen people, trumpet mediumship comes to mind. Revelation also makes references to the use of trumpets in Chapter 1, verse 10, and Chapter 4, verse 1. In the end, Paul said, "the last enemy that will be abolished is death."

It would be a while before fear of death was tackled. Following the Roman persecution of the Christians, the movement had to go underground, as knowledge had to be kept secret or occult. Ironically, in the 1500s, it was the Christian church which became the persecutor severely punishing those who practiced divination. Nostradamus, (1503-1566) lived in constant fear of the Inquisition. Secretly in his upstairs study, he managed to employ the art of scrying. Eventually he published the first of his *Centuries* in 1555. The Prince of Prophets successfully predicted the French Revolution, the rise of Napoleon, the one he termed the first Antichrist, and a second Antichrist, called Hisler—misspelling Hilter's name by one letter! However, it would take three hundred years before modern Spiritualism emerged as a religious movement whose central task was to dispel what Paul called the last enemy—death.

Chapter Two:
Modern Spiritualism

"Environment modifies life but does not govern life. The soul is stronger than its surroundings."

—William James

Modern Spiritualism began with physical mediumship—spirit raps to be specific. In 1847, the Fox family moved into a cottage that had been a site for previous spiritual rapping. Soon ten-year-old Kate Fox and her sister, Maggie, seven, were communicating with the sprit of a dead peddler, whom the girls dubbed, "Mr. Split-foot." Through a series of coded raps, a story emerged. The spirit told the sisters that he had been murdered and his body buried ten feet below the ground in the basement of the cottage.[1] Later, when the cellar was dug up, human bones and the tin box of an itinerant peddler, Charles Rosna, were found corroborating the story. The peddler's tin box is now on display in the Museum at Lily Dale Assembly in New York.

Not surprisingly, the two sisters soon were the talk of their small community of Hydesville, New York. Everyone wanted to see the young mediums. On November 14, 1849, the girls made their first public appearance in Corinthian Hall, Rochester, New York. Kate and Maggie Fox became an instant success by demonstrating their ability to communicate with spirit. Soon, their older sister, Leah, became a secretary for Kate and Maggie Fox as they traveled the country demonstrating spirit communication. Audiences adored the handsome sisters with their shapely figures and brunette beauty.

All three sisters married wealthy husbands. In 1852, Maggie married Dr. Elisha Kane, the famous Artic explorer, and in 1858, Leah married wealthy businessman David Underhill. Later, Kate married a British barrister in 1872, a choice that so pleased spirit that raps loudly echoed from the wooded altar as the couple said their vows. In fact, the Fox sisters seem to attract favorable reviews wherever they demonstrated mediumship. William Crookes, who examined Kate Fox over a period, proclaimed her "the most wonderful living medium."[1]

Unfortunately, mediumship, travel, and constant scrutiny took its toll on Maggie and Kate Fox. Emma Hardinge Britten described the arduous work of Kate: "Poor patient Kate in the midst of capricious, grumbling crowds of investigators, repeating hour after hour the letters of the alphabet, while a less poor patient spirit rapped out names, ages, and dates to suit all comers."[2] Often, the girls endured the humiliation of strip searches from suspicious researchers as well as jeers from non-believers.

Unfortunately, marriage provided little security for Kate and Maggie. Maggie called herself Mrs. Kane and resided with her "husband." However, when Dr. Kane died, she was left penniless—his family claiming the couple were never legally wed. Kate's husband also died young, leaving her with two young children to support.

Sadly, both Kate and Maggie Fox developed penchant for drink, much to their older sister's dismay. Leah, staunch Spiritualist, tried in a vain attempt to reform them by calling public attention to their behavior. Things got uglier. Leah tried to have Kate's children removed on the grounds that she was an unfit mother. Not surprisingly, Maggie and Kate fought back. To spite the faithful Leah, they claimed their mediumship was nothing but a fraud. The raps, in fact, were perpetrated by cracking their toes. The deliberate lie was for the express purpose of embarrassing both the Spiritualist movement and their sister, Leah, one of its most devote supporters. The die was cast. Even when Maggie Fox tried to retract her story in the *New York Tribune* a year later in November 1889. The spirit, however, did not dessert Maggie Fox. Even on her death-bed, in 1893, rappings were heard: "According to the doctor (Dr. Mellen), she (Maggie Fox) was unable at the time, to move hand or foot. Yet knockings came from the wall, the floor, and the ceiling in response to Margaretta's faint questions."[3]

Spiritualism, however shaky its beginnings, has continued to progress in the second half of the nineteenth century. Even President Lincoln invited medium, Nettie Colburn Maynard, to the White House. During the Civil War, Mrs. Lincoln introduced the medium to the president after the death of their son, Willie. During one White House séance, the spirit of General Knox, the first Secretary of War, gave Lincoln this advise on how to wage war: "Less note of preparation. Less policy talk. More action!"[4] Nettie Colburn Maynard also claimed that the outline for the Emancipation Proclamation was given directly through spirit!

Spiritualism was popular, not only with those in power, but the common folk as well. Horace Greeley (1811-1872), an American journalist, opened columns in his newspapers for those who wished to write on spirit communications. Professor J. S. Loveland wrote the first American book on Spiritualism, Esoteric Truths of Spiritualism, bringing the Spiritualism to the masses, while missionaries such Dr. James Peebles (1822-1922), traveled the world lecturing on spirit communication. Peebles, who was both a medical doctor and a Universalist minister wrote many books including *What is Spiritualism?* and *Seers Through the Ages*. Emma Hardings Britten went on to found the Spiritualist publication, *Two Worlds*.

The most famous physical medium of the day was Daniel Douglas Home (1831-1886). From the age of nineteen, Home had the ability to levitate to the degree that he could levitate out one third-story window and into the next, while visiting England's Lord Adler. His many admirers included, Elizabeth Barrett Browning and Lord Adare. To the dismay of critics, such as Robert Browning, scientist William Crookes tested and validated Home's mediumship.

William Crookes also studied the mediumship of Florence Cook, whose control, the spirit of a young girl named Katie King, would materialize. While Katie King did not speak, she smiled, and even shook hands or sat on the lap of a participant in the séance. Even when others claimed her fraudulent, Crookes remained steadfast in his support of Cook.

While Sir William Crookes researched Florence Cook in England, Dr. William James investigated medium Lenore Piper in the

United Sates, introducing the medium to the American Society for Psychical Research. James, who later penned, *Varieties of Religious Experience*, was unwavering in his faith: "I have a firm conviction that most of the phenomena of psychic research are rooted in reality."

Sir Arthur Connan Doyle (1858-1930), a celebrated author, was another champion of psychic phenomena. He introduced his then friend, Harry Houdini, to spiritualism. Later, Houdini wrote *A Magician Among the Spirits*, a book that was to end their friendship. The great magician explained: "Sir Arthur thinks I have great mediumistic powers and that some of my feats are done with the aid of spirits. Everything I do is accomplished by materials—means humanly possible, no matter how baffling to the layman."

However, Houdini did meet his match when he was introduced to Boston medium, Margery Cranston. Cranston, who took no money for her séances, produced incredible phenomena which included direct voice, trumpet mediumship, table tipping, and finger-printing of spirit fingers, as well as writing in Chinese calligraphy while in trance. Her control was the spirit of her deceased brother, Walter, who communicated to sitters via a trumpet which levitated around the circle. Houdini wagered his $1,000 judge's fee that Margery Crandon was a fraud. It is rumored that Houdini was so anxious to prove the medium a fake, he had his assistant plant a folding rumor in Crandon's cabinet. James Collins, a former assistant of Houdini's, claimed this to be true many years later.

Before his untimely death from a ruptured appendix, Houdini made a pact with his wife, Beatrice. If communication was possible from the other side, Houdini promised to get a message through to Beatrice. According to Reverend Arthur Ford, Houdini kept his promise. In *Unknown, But Known*, Reverend Ford tells how as a young pastor of the First Spiritualist Church of Manhattan, said that the spirit of Harry Houdini came to him. Soon, the Spiritualist medium arranged a séance date with Houdini's widow. During the 1929 séance, Ford brought through a coded message, that Beatrice Houdini later verified came form Harry Houdini, and she signed a letter to this fact.

Houdini may not have been as much of a skeptic as people thought, for he did have at least one reading with Edgar Cayce, according to Cayce biographer Sidney Kirkpatrick. Edgar Cayce (1877-1945) was a remarkable medical clairvoyant. In trance, Cayce is credited with saving his infant nephew, Tommy House, his young wife, Gertrude from TB, and their son, Hugh Lynn's eye sight. Cayce's guides advocated drugless methods of healing and a positive attitude.

In the 1920s, Cayce met Arthur Lammars, a wealthy printer interested in metaphysics. Soon Cayce's readings included remarks on astrology and reincarnation and Jesus. According to The Source, Jesus represented the model for humanity. Harry Houdini, Eileen Garrett, Nicolai Tesler, Thomas Edison, and Gloria Swanson all sought his advice, as well as President Woodrow Wilson. According to noted writer Harwood Bro, Cayce was instructed to come alone to the White House. Bro further states that Cayce gave directions for the League of Nations during one trance session for President Wilson.

Years later, another psychic was called to the White House. In her autobiography, seer Jeanne Dixon, told how she smuggled her crystal ball into the White House in 1944. When President Roosevelt asked how long he had to live, Mrs. Dixon peered into the crystal ball and replied, "Not long." The President died within the year. Later, Jeanne Dixon predicted a Democrat would win the 1960 election, but would die in office. Sadly, her forecast came true when John F. Kennedy, a Democrat was elected in 1960 and was assassinated in November 1963.

Interest in psychics and mediumship flourished in the 1960s, as did the big Spiritualist Camps—Camp Lily Dale in New York, Camp Cassadaga in Florida, and Camp Chesterfield in Indiana. Psychic phenomena seemed to have exploded, with the advent of New Age consciousness. *A Course in Miracles* became popular along with the Seth books channeled by Jane Roberts. In the 1980s and 90s, channeler, J. Z. Knight founded Ramtha's School of Enlightenment. Channeling became increasingly popular. Channeler Paul Solomon became known as the second Edgar Cayce, and Jack Burek channeled Lazaris to packed auditoriums. Premiere channeler Elwood Babbitt produced three books in trance *Talks with Christ, Testament of the Vishnu,* and *Perfect Health.* Other popular channelers, Lee Carroll, Gordon Michael Scallion, and Sean David Morton put out their own newsletters. Many mediums, such as John Roberts, Sylvia Browne, and James Van Praagh are seen regularly on television. In fact, Mediumship is so hot, there are two television programs based on it—*Medium* and *Ghost Whisperer.* Few mediums, though, have the gift of physical mediumship. Only one truly great physical medium comes to mind—Reverend Hoyt Robinette of Chesterfield, Indiana. In fact, physical mediumship is shunned at many of the Spiritualist Camps. Camp Lily Dale even goes as far as to ban physical mediumship. Why? The official reply is because there are too many mediums who have "faked" physical phenomena, so that Lily Dale leaders just threw up their hands and banned all physical mediumship.

Both camps—Lily Dale and Chesterfield—are active. Lily Dale, established in 1879, is billed as the largest Spiritualist camp in the world—a village with its own post office, Volunteer Fire Department, the Karma Café, a huge auditorium with several lecture halls, a healing chapel, two hotels, and a museum. In the museum, there are artifacts such as the peddler's box, the Fox family's *Bible,* precipitated spirit painting by the Bangs sisters and the Campbell brothers, slates by famous mediums with messages and drawings, as well early Spiritualist literature and scrapbooks. "The detail precipitated paintings of the Bangs sisters and the Campbell brothers is amazing," explained Ron Nagy from behind the counter at the Lily Dale Museum. "Only spirit would take so much care in drawing an eye. Most artists would not put that much effort in drawing the iris."

Spirit seems to be everywhere at Lily Dale. Joyce La Judice, who runs the hotel, relates this story of independent voice at the Lily Dale Spiritualist Church service: While waiting to go up on stage, Reverend Betty Putnam's independent voice started speaking—it seemed to be coming from Betty's solar plexus. You could hear every word they were saying. Betty looked down and asked spirit, "Are you going to give the lecture or am I?" Joyce also clairvoyantly saw a lady in a long white dress coming down the stairs.

It was Cora Richmond, a fact verified when Joyce later she saw a picture of Cora in the same outfit.[6]

Spirit is especially strong in Assembly Hall where daily lectures are delivered by ardent Spiritualists. Pictures of mediums from the past line the walls. Several times, when I was lecturing at Lily Dale, I have felt their eyes literally watching me as I delivered a talk on "Dreams and Astral Travel" or "Soul Cycles." Just walking around the grounds, spirit people dressed in Victorian attire can be observed clairvoyantly. It seems like the atmosphere there is three deep with spirit! Also, the energy above the Assembly Hall which houses visiting mediums is alive with spirit. More than once, I have captured orbs or mists on photos of the halls and living room above Assembly Hall. I have been awakened by more than one visit from an early morning spirit, when spending the night at Lily Dale!

Another Spiritualist camp which I have visited is Camp Chesterfield in Indiana. Unlike Lily Dale which avoids physical mediumship, Chesterfield mediums embrace all forms of mediumship, including trumpet séances—and its manifestation—sometimes to the camp's detriment. For example, during the 1960s, when the demand for physical phenomena was at its peak, many fraudulent mediums came on the scene. One of the most slick was Lamar Keene. Sadly, Keene's glib manner and slight-of-hand tricks made him one of Camp Chesterfield's most popular up-and-coming mediums. Apparently, Keene *did* have a smidgeon of psychic ability, as he was able to locate a will for a wealthy widow by saying the first thing that popped into his mind. The grateful woman later legally adopted the adult medium. However, the rest of his work as outlined in *Psychic Mafia* was pure flim-flam. On a positive note, the book did help open the eyes of Chesterfield officials to fraudulent mediums on the grounds.

When I visited Camp Chesterfield in April 2005, I was so impressed with Reverend Suzanne Greer's trumpet séance, I returned in July with several students from the New England School of Metaphysics. We took lessons in trumpet mediumship with Reverend Greer and trance mediumship with Reverend Patricia Kennedy. The highlight our the visit was Reverend Hoyt Robinette's spirit card séance. I had just completed *Connecticut Ghosts*. I was able to obtain permission to use all the pictures I wanted in the book save one—that of Reverend Carl Hewitt. I was totally dumb-founded when I looked at the spirit card (page 31) I received in July 2005. There was a picture of Carl Hewitt (page 30) just below the face of famed medium Clifford Bias. The lime and rust colors were also evident, as they are the same colors as the cover of *Connecticut Ghosts*. As I told Reverend Hoyt Robinette, "It is a card that I truly treasure."

Andrew Jackson Davis (1826-1910). Courtesy of Prints and Photographs Division, Library of Congress.

Kate and Maggie Fox.
Courtesy of Missouri
Historical Society.

Reverend Carl R.
Hewitt. Courtesy of
Sidney Schwartz.

Spirit Card produced at séance given by Reverend Hoyt Robinette. The card manifested in the exact same colors of *Connecticut Ghosts*, even though the cover had not yet been created.

Chapter Three:
Physical Mediumship

J. Malcolm Bird, managing editor of the Scientific American *declared in an address before the Medill School of Journalism that psychic phenomena genuinely exist. "There are real 'spirit voices' though we have no proof that they are spirits," he said. "There are genuine clairvoyants who can see pictures of the past, present and future. There are spirit writings which display power far beyond the ability of the writer. And there are even more surprising genuine phenomena in the field of the objective or physical manifestations."*
—Boston Journal February 18, 1924

The National Spiritualist Association of churches awards two mediumship certificates—one for mental mediumship and the other for physical mediumship. Sylvia Browne, James Van Praagh, and George Anderson are examples of mental mediums. Each relies on telepathy, clairvoyance, and clairaudience to contact spirit. Telepathy or mind to mind communication is the most common approach to communicate with the spirit of loved ones, contact spirit guides and doctors, as well as provide inspiration for art, music, and literature. In fact, for many artists, it is so natural that they do not even realize that they are receiving inspiration from the other side! Next, with gifts of clairvoyance (French for clear seeing) and clairaudience (French for clear hearing), the medium can literally hear and see spirit objectively outside or subjectively in the mind's eye.

In mental mediumship, the individual relies upon the mind or mental processes for the purposes of communication with spirit. Physical mediumship, on the other hand, involves the production of phenomena which can be experienced through one of the physical human senses by all present. Physical mediums have been known to produce a wide variety of physical manifestations—table tipping, raps, levitation, transfiguration, apports, materialization, trumpet séances, independent or direct voice slate writing, and even precipitated paintings. Examples of physical mediums include Kate and Maggie Fox, D. D. Home, Florence Cook, Emily French, Margery Crandon, and the Bangs Sisters. All had very special gifts. Kate and Maggie Fox communicated with raps which were heard by all present.

D. D. Home possessed the unique gift of levitation which all could view. Both Emily French and Margery Crandon had the ability to do independent or direct voice mediumship in which spirit could be heard distinctly from different parts of the room by those within earshot. Margery Crandon also was able to do trumpet séances in which the trumpet levitates and acts as a megaphone for spirit communication. In Florence Cook's séance room, spirit not only spoke, but materialized in full figure. Katie King, one of Cook's guides, was photographed several times. Spirit even has the ability to write on slate or cards.

The museums at Lily Dale Assembly and Camp Chesterfield contain many examples of slates with spirit messages written in chalk. Even more fascinating are the many portraits done by the Bangs sister, accomplished mediums who were able to precipitate painting—a process by which a picture precipitates or materializes on canvas.

During the early days of spiritualism, table tipping and raps were the rage. Spirits literally rapped out names, dates, and answers to questions as the Fox sisters remained seated on stage. Kate Fox's mediumship was investigated by William Crookes and passed with flying colors. Later, D. D. Home, Florence Cook, the Eddy brothers, and the Bangs sisters also demonstrated their abilities before scientific minds.

Perhaps the best documented case of physical mediumship was that of Daniel Douglas Home. Born in Scotland, March 20, 1833, Home emigrated to the United States when he was nine. At nineteen, Home experienced his first levitation. His family thought he was demonic; he was forced to leave his home.

D. D. Home continued to win over skeptics with his exceptional abilities. When tested by two Harvard researchers, Home's gifts were pronounced as genuine psychic powers. Home, who never charged for a sitting, gave the most extraordinary séances: "His sitters were frequently privileged to witness the most astounding events, often in good light—levitation of tables and other objects, playing of musical instruments by unseen hands and actual materialization of spirit hands and so forth."[1]

D. D. Home became known for his levitations. In fact, on several occasions, he levitated out one upper story window and back into the room through an adjoining window. One levitation on December 13, 1868, was witnessed by Lord Adare and Lord Lindsay: "In 1868, Home produced his most famous levitation at the home of Lord Adare. He went into trance and reportedly floated out a window on the third floor, then floated back in another window. The same year he handled red-hot coals and stuck his head into a fire without being burned."[2]

Home gave an estimated fifteen hundred séances, which included spirit communication as well as physical phenomena. When he died of tuberculosis in 1886, he left a legacy of levitation and materialization for the world to ponder. He also left the world with a good reputation—never once had D. D. Home been proven a fraud.

Another physical medium, known for materializations, did not fare as well. Florence Cook (1856 – 1904) is reported to effect full materializations of her controls— most notably the child, Katie King. Like D. D. Home, Florence Cook's gifts were not well received in the beginning. She lost her job as a teacher due to the poltergeist activity in the classroom. However, Florence Cook continued to develop as a physical medium to the point where the spirit of Katie King materialized. Cook was so secure in her abilities, that she invited reporters from the *Daily Telegraph* to witness the materialization. The report in the newspaper, dated October 10, 1872, stated that the reporter saw faces during the séance, and on August 12, 1873, he was able to take a picture of Katie King! As Florence Cook's reputation grew, scientist Sir William Crookes investigated her work with very favorable results. His reports in the *Spiritualist* dated April 1874, noted: "Katie never appeared to greater perfection and for nearly two hours she walked around the room, conversing familiarly with those present." At one séance, the spirit of Katie King sat on the lap of a sitter who felt a light-weight child, and at another she allowed a sitter to cut a piece of her dress.

Such materializations would be a difficult fraud to pull off in any circumstance, let alone when the best scientific minds of the country were present. Unfortunately, a scandal ensued when Crookes, a sincere investigator of Spiritualism, was rumored to be romantically involved with Florence Cook. While Crookes' personal involvement with Florence Cook cast a shadow on his investigation, many others witnessed Katie King's spirit materialize, while the medium was sitting in her cabinet in deep trance with her hands behind her back. Whoever Katie King was, she definitely was not Florence Cook in disguise, as some claimed, since Katie King bore no resumblance to her medium. After Katie King departed, other spirit girls came in to assist—Leila, Florence, and Marie. All exhibited different builds, mannerism, and personalities. Florence Cook continued doing séances until her death in 1904.

Even more spectacular materializations were taking place in the United States. While Florence Cook was working in England, the Eddy brothers were materializing spirits in Chittenden, Vermont, a town seven miles north of Rutland. Colonel Henry Steele Olcott, a lawyer who spoke several languages, was sent to investigate the brothers in August of 1874. He returned to the Eddy farmhouse many times thereafter, documenting their extraordinary gifts in his 1875 book, *People From the Other World*. It was also at the Eddy farm that he met Madame Blavatsky. The two later became famous as the founders of the Theosophical Society.

Colonel Olcutt's first impression of the two brothers was far from favorable, as detailed in *People from the Other World*: "The brothers, Horatio and William, who are the present mediums, are sensitive, distant, and curt to strangers, look more like hard-working rough farmers than prophets or priests of the new dispensation, have black hair and eyes, stiff joints, a clumsy carriage, shrink form advances and make new-comers feel ill at ease and unwelcome." He was later to confirm that the brothers were the most amazing mediums in the country—their distrustful personalities were due to the unkindness of their neighbors. The country folk saw them as diabolical. Even their own father, Zaphaniah Eddy, did not take to their trances, and many time tried to starve and beat the evil spirits out of them.

Fortunately for the brothers, their mother, Julia, was also mediumistic. Her great- great-great grandmother, Mary Bradley, convicted of witch craft by a Salem court in 1692, fled to her native Scotland. All of her ten children, with the exception of her eldest son, John, inherited her ability. The Eddy children grew up with spirit manifestation, disembodied faces and hands, spirit voices and rappings. Deaths in the family were often preceded by ghostly apparitions. The vision of a royal Scottish lady in a coach announced the death of Mrs. Eddy's mother. A week before James Eddy died of diphtheria, a lady on a white horse came to visit him, and a day before Miranda Eddy died, a bell appeared over her head and tolled twice![4]

After their father died in 1872, the brothers felt free to built a circle-room in which to conduct their direct voice séances. These séances drew the attention of many, including Colonel Olcutt. In an article, "The Mediumistic Gifts of the Eddy Family in General," he lists their gifts as follows: "rappings, the disturbance of a slate at rest; painting in oil and water-colors under influence; prophecy, the speaking in strange tongues, healing gift; the discernment of spirits; levitation or the floating of the body in free air; the phenomena of instrument-playing and the showing of hands; the writing of messages on paper up-bourne in mid-air, by pencil held by detached hands; psychometry or the reading of character view of distant persons upon touching sealed letters; clairvoyance; clairaudience' or the hearing of spirit-voices; and lastly, and most miraculous of all, the materialization of phantom forms, that become visible, tangible and audible by all persons present." The spirits not only materialized but wrote their names on cards and played instruments before the eyes of the amazed sitters![5]

Olcutt was very precise in his investigation. He even took time to measure spirits. Honto, a young Indian spirit girl who was exactly five foot, three inches tall; Santum a male, measured six foot, three inches tall. At one séance, according to Olcutt, Honto allowed Mrs. Cleveland to cut a lock of her hair and even smoked a pipe! The American Indian spirits loved to do their ceremonial dances. Colonel Olcutt described their antics as follows: "There is a dance of howling, leaping, skylarking Indians, who beat on drums, rattle the tambourines, blow the horns, ring the heavier bells, and make a din so hideous one easily fancies himself caught in the dance of live redskins about starting on the war path." All this occurred while the mediums remained bound in their cabinets!

When Madame Helena Petrova Blavatsky arrived at the Eddy Homestead on October 14, 1874, some very interesting spirits materialized. According to Olcutt, when the curtain lifted, a spirit appeared uttering, "Djadja," Russian for *uncle*. It was Madame Blavatsky's uncle, M. Gustave Hahn, a past president of the Criminal Court in Russia who had died in 1861. Next the spirit of her old family nurse addressed her with the same endearments given in childhood. A Hindu coolie and an Arab athlete brought greetings, as well as the spirit of Hassan Agha, an old family friend. Last, but not least, her materialized uncle brought her an apport—the silver buckle which had been buried with her father, along with his medals from a Russian tomb over 5,000 miles away![6]

The Eddy Brothers were not as kind to Harry Houdini, who was turned away at the door due to a full house. Both brothers continued to hold séances after their most public years of 1874 to 1878. Horatio Eddy died in 1922, and William Eddy passed over in 1932.

Emily French (1831 to 1912) also demonstrated extraordinary physical mediumship at the turn of the century. Known for her direct voice mediumship, she was investigated thoroughly by Edward C. Randall, a prominent lawyer. Randall held over 700 séances with Emily French from 1890 to 1912 which he details in his five books. During these séances, which took place in upstate New York, spirits were heard giving their personal messages as well as answering questions on death and the other side. The guide explained that there were seven spheres—the lowest reserved for earth-bound spirits. When ready to receive help, there were hospitals and homes on the side. However, the guides explained, "There is no advancement for such men or any man until the desire comes from within."

When asked how one could advance, the spirit guide explained that thoughts built character: Every wrong acted on earth must be lived over here, and lived right before one can progress. If your world knew this fact, incentive to wrong would be counteracted, so you would have a better world and a happier people. As you are developing character, every hour of your earth life, you see how important it is to build it right.[6]

Just as fascinating as Emily French's direct voice mediumship was the spirit painting of the Bangs sisters who also demonstrated clairvoyance, physical manifestation, and direct voice mediumship. Lizzie and May Bangs, however, are best remembered for "precipitated" spirit portraits. While sitting in the room with a blank canvas, the background, figures, and finally details of a portrait would manifest frequently resembling the face of a deceased relative! Most, like Mrs. Gertrude Bresian Hunt, did not take their eyes from the canvas: "I did not remove my eyes from the canvas, and would stake everything I possess that no hand touch the canvas after I placed it in the bright light of the window, until the picture was finished."

The sisters, who grew up in a average family at the turn of the century in Chicago, were born mediums. Their first manifestation was pieces of coal. When they were five, rapping and voices from beyond were heard. Later came physical manifestations, automatic writing, independent slate writing, clairvoyance, and clairaudience. By the early 1900s, the young mediums were manifesting excellent likenesses of deceased relatives in about twenty minutes to three hours without ever touching the canvas. For example, Dr. Daughtery received a portrait of his deceased wife, Lizzie, and later requested his twin daughters, who were also in spirit, to appear. He also obtained a portrait of his deceased father who had died fourteen years earlier. There were other supernatural occurrences as well. For example, in a portrait of baby "Bernal Tobias," the painted eyes of the baby opened and shut, then remained opened, according to startled observers.

Their slate séances were also fascinating. In *Glimpses of the Next State*, Admiral W. Usborne Moore describes a 1908 slate séance with Miss May Bangs. He brought along his questions in a sealed envelop and placed the envelop, which also contained several numbered sheets of blank paper, between two slates tied together with rubber bands. After a half hour of conversation, the séance ended with three raps from the slates. Miss Bangs then opened the slates and gave him back his envelope, still sealed. Admiral Moore was quite surprised when he slit opened the envelope: "The replies were categorical, giving or confirming information of great value to me personally; referring to facts and happening of forty years ago, which the spirit and I alone were aware of; and adding the names of individuals whom I had not named in my questions, but whom we both knew in the past, and who had participated in the events referred to by me. The reply to the fifth and last question was in the form of greeting from spirit friends who were known to me when they were in earth life, and now come as so called "guides."

Physical mediumship, which was so popular in the Victorian Era, seemed to go out of vogue for a while. However, during the last part of 1800s, three remarkable physical mediums were born one in Ontario, Canada—Margery Crandon in 1881, and two in England—Helen Duncan in 1887 and Estelle Roberts in 1889.

Many considered Margery Crandon (1888 to 1941) to be the last of the great physical mediums in the United States. She became a medium without much thought. Her second husband, Dr. Leroi Crandon had read about the success of home circles such as the Golighter Circle abroad. He became fascinated with the subject and decided to try table tipping with a group of six. Soon, it was discovered that the table only moved when Margery was present. Realizing his wife's potential as a medium, Dr. Crandon encouraged her development. She developed rapidly from levitation of a table under red light, to trance, trumpet and direct voice mediumship.

Even when Margery's mouth was filled with liquid or marbles, the spirit voice of Walter could be heard clearly from different parts of the laboratory. She also was able to join three solid wooden rings together under test conditions and write in ancient Chinese calligraphy while in trance.

Margery Crandon's phenomenal physical mediumship did not escape public attention. At one point, *Scientific America*, had decided to award her a prize of $2,500 after she successfully submitted to investigations by their committee, as well as investigators from the American Society for Psychical Research. Word of her success quickly spread to England. When Arthur Findley came over from England to research Margery's physical mediumship, he proclaimed her: "the eighth wonder of the world!" What happened to this talented medium is a travesty of justice. On July 23, 1923, Margery, the committee of judges from *Scientific American* again tested her mediumship. She passed all tests. In the first test, she successfully rang a bell with her arms and legs strapped down, proving she could move matter. Next, she went into trance and showed her ability to conduct a trumpet séance. The spirit of her deceased brother, Walter, came through and spoke clearly through the trumpet. When Walter asked his sister where he should move the trumpet, Houdini, one of the judges, spoke up and said, "Over here." The trumpet then made a nose-dive to Houdini—an inauspicious move. Was Margery worried? Not really. Her guides had encouraged her to face her rival honestly. They even claimed that Houdini's number was up—which turned out to be true as he died a few years later.

What Margery's guides did not count on was deceit! In the final test, Margery was placed in a specially constructed cabinet and Walter was asked to ring the bell. This time the bell did not ring. Walter accused Houdini of planting a ruler in the cabinet to discredit his sister. When a ruler was found, Margery's mediumship came into question. Only years later did Houdini's assistant, Jim Collins admit to planting it there: "I chucked it in the box myself. The boss told me to do it. He wanted to fix her good."[7] While many loyal supporters, such as Sir Arthur Conan Doyle, continued to support Margery's mediumship, others such as Dr. J. B. Rhine publically did not.

Another great physical medium, Helen Duncan, faced similar trials and was even prosecuted for her physical mediumship. Many Spiritualist considered her a martyr to the cause. Few mediums have ever possessed her remarkable ability to materialize spirits. It was her spirit guide, Dr. Williams, who told her to build a cabinet to gather ectoplasm for materialization and to obtain a trumpet and a red light for the séances. In the 1930s and 40s, Helen gave a weekly séance at the Master Temple in Portsmouth, England. Unfortunately, Helen was fined for fraudulent mediumship in 1931—even though her control, Albert Stewart, had tried in vain to warn her. She continued her mediumship with remarkable evidence of spirit survival.

Later, during World War II, a young sailor with H. M. S. Barnum on his cap materialized before his surprised mother, saying, "Mum the ship was sank and we were all killed." Winston Churchill was incensed at this breach of security and ordered Helen prosecuted. The military tried her under the archaic 1737 Witchcraft Act. Helen Duncan was sentenced to six months in jail. Unfortunately, this remarkable medium was under police investigation right up until her death on December 6, 1956.

Estelle Roberts, who worked during the same period, had a more cordial relationship with the British police. In 1937, Roberts through her guide, made contact with the spirit of a missing ten-year-old child, Mona Tinsley, by holding an item of her clothing. Estelle Roberts explained: "As I took it (clothing) from its wrappings, I knew at once Mona was dead. Just then my old dog who had been sleeping leapt to his feet and began to career madly around the room." Mona's spirit went on to describe the house in which she was strangled. When the police drove Estelle Roberts around the city, the medium pointed out the murderer's home and the police were able to apprehend the child's killer.

Her physical mediumship was equally astounding. On one occasion, her guide, Red Cloud, requested that two plaques and a red torch be placed in the séance cabinet. Maurice Barbanell describes what happened next in *Psychic News:* "Within a short time the two plaques rose up and Red Cloud's silhouette could be seen." Red Cloud allowed the sitters to examine him and then proceeded to demonstrate his remarkable ability. "Following this, *an extraordinary spectacle* took place. This was when the cabinet curtains were parted and the materialized person held the torch to illuminate another. After this the trumpets moved and apports were produced through them. Each sitter received one, and most were given a jewel. Barbanell asked Red Cloud where they came from and laughingly, he replied, *The Land of Anywhere.*"[8] Estelle Roberts wrote her autobiography in 1959, *Fifty Years a Medium,* and continued her remarkable mediumship until her death in 1970.

Leslie Flint, who called himself "the most tested medium in England," also left a legacy of spirit communication. Flint began his direct voice mediumship in 1935. With the help of his main guide Mickey, he brought through the voices of the so-called dead—some of whom had been quite well-known in life. These messages can be heard on LeslieFlint.com. The following message was received from Mahatma Ghandi: "The first lesson one must learn is to forget oneself, to give out in love all that is possible from within yourself, and it shall be returned to you. These things that Christ spoke about, and all the great teachers, all the great philosophers down through the ages, was that man should forget himself, so that in return he might find himself."

While Leslie Flint had a long career as a direct voice medium, Jack Webber's career was relatively brief. He demonstrated time and again his ability to materialize apports, levitate heavy tables, materialize ectoplasm, which included direct voice and ectoplasm in the 1930s and 40s. In a biography of Webber, Harry Edwards describes Weber's voices as they emanated from the trumpet: "Clearly, too without such force, Paddy (a boy control) is often heard, as is also the rich contralto voice of a lady, and other spirit singers. A phenomenon (impossible for human agency to reproduce) is the singing of Reuben and Paddy at the same time through the same trumpet." In addition to the levitation of the trumpet, veils of ectoplasm appeared and tables weighing forty-five pounds lifted into mid air—all captured on infrared film. Sometimes, even the medium's jacket was turned inside out by playful spirits while he was in trance. Unfortunately, Webber's mediumship was short-lived as he passed over to the spirit side of life at age thirty-three, just as his mediumship was becoming public.[9]

America has also had great trance channelers. One of the most celebrated is Edgar Cayce, dubbed "the Sleeping Prophet." Edgar Cayce channeled the archangels Michael and Gabriel. Harmon Bro once described to an ARE (Association for Research and Englightment) audience one such session. Those who sat in on one reading with Michael felt the atmosphere was charged with energy. Each of the sitters saw the others taking on a finer, more perfected appearance. The archangel Michael, who first appeared during a lesson, entitled "Open Door" in September 1932, gave this advice:

"BE STILL MY CHILDREN! Bow thy heads that the Lord of the Way may make known unto you that you have been chosen for a service within this period when there is need of that spirit being manifest on earth. (You who have) named the name make known thy daily walks of life, in the little acts of the lessons that have been builded into thy experiences, through those associations of self in meditation and prayer that his way may be known among them: for He calls on all whosoever will may come... for today will yet harken, the way is open, I MICHAEL CALL ON THEE."[10]

Edgar Cayce also had some unusual physical manifestations when he and Mitchell Hastings went out West in 1934 in search of relaxation. Mitchell Hastings, a young college student at the time, was an electrical genius who received early admission at Harvard University. He and Edgar Cayce were close enough in the desert to see these visions: An apparition of Cayce's dead mother appeared and spoke to Cayce about the future. She urged him not to give up hope and not to worry about his precarious financial situation. Not to doubt the power and veracity of the information coming through him. In previous visionary experiences, Edgar had only seen or heard spirit visitors, but here in New Mexico, perhaps aided by Hastings's own power of mind, Edgar reportedly received a physical manifestation of the visit. His mother handed him a silver dollar, and when she faded from sight, the coin remained in the palm of his hand.[11] The same silver dollar was later passed on to Hugh Lynn Cayce, his oldest son.

Unfortunately, Edgar Cayce's work was not researched by scientists. Cayce simply wasn't interested. The one time he *was* tested, a doubting researcher cut his toenail off while Cayce was in deep trance, causing the medium great pain when he awakened. Cayce decided not to venture into scientific hands again!

Another medium, Eileen Garrett, however was very much interested in being tested by scientists. In fact, Mrs. Garrett came into prominence with an extraordinary séance set up by the National Laboratory of Psychical Research under the auspices of Harry Price. Their purpose was to make contact with Arthur Connan Doyle. When Eileen Garrett went into trance, she made contact not only with Doyle, but Flight Lieutenant H. Carmichael Irwin, who had died in a dirigible crash in France a few days earlier. In precise detail, the spirit of Lieutenant Irwin explained the cause of the crash of *R 101*. "Engines too heavy. It was this that made me on five occasions scuttle to safety."

Later, Mrs. Garrett came to the United States where she was researched by Dr. J. D. Rhine with favorable results. She respected researchers and founded the Parapsychology Foundation in New York City, remaining active in research and hosting annual symposiums on parapsychology until her death in 1970. Her legacy, the Parapsychology Foundation, remains active today under the guidance of her daughter, Eileen Coly and granddaughter, Lisette Coly.

One of the finest American Spiritualist mediums was the late Arthur Ford. Ford discovered his gift in World War I, when he would see the names of the dead soldiers in his sleep, before their names were posted. His guide, Fletcher, was a Canadian soldier who had died during the war. Interested in meditation, Ford had studied briefly with Paramahansa Yogananda, but the world of Spiritualism was his real calling.

At a time when most mediums provided only first names of the so-called dead, Reverend Ford gave first and last names of the deceased with equal ease. After he gained national recognition with his Houdini séance, Ford continued his work as a Spiritualist medium, giving readings to other famous men, such as the Reverend Sun Myung Moon. One of his most spectacular séances with Reverend Sun Myung Moon occurred on March 18, 1965, when Fletcher brought through the names of "Colonel Kousik, a deceased Korean statesman and " Kim Koo," a martyred patriot from Korea. Fletcher said this about Reverend Moon: "This man has a message—this man has a message—but the Holy Spirit, the Spirit of Truth, can speak through Moon more clearly, more completely—than he is able to speak through any one individual today." Fletcher closed the reading with this caveat: "But never make the mistake of associating the truth which flows from any man, through any man, of identifying it completely with that man. The Spirit of Truth uses men, it is not a man." Ford later gave the first televised séance bringing through the son of Bishop Pike on Canadian television and was active in Spiritual Frontiers, a group he helped to establish. Arthur Ford was just as active in spirit as he was in life. After his death in 1971, Ruth Montgomery, the veteran newspaper writer, began receiving messages from Ford which she detailed in her book, *A World Beyond.*

Great literature, art, and music all have been channeled through spirit. One spirit, Patience Worth, channeled award-winning plays and poetry. In 1913, Pearl Curran, a St. Louis housewife, was playing with the Ouija Board™ with her two friends, when the pointer spelled out this message: "Many moons ago I lived. Again I come. Patience Worth is my name." For twenty-four years Patience Worth continued to visit Mrs. Curran. During that period, the spirit dictated seven full-length books and thousands of poems. One literary critic termed one book, "the greatest story of the life and times of Christ since the Gospels were penned."

Patience Worth took a personal interest in Pearl Curran's life encouraging her to adopt a baby girl—named Patience Wee. When John Curran, Pearl's husband died in 1922, Patience dedicated this poem to him which was read at his memorial:

These are things I have laid down: Sorrow, doubt, confusion.
These things I have taken up: Labor, love, understanding.
He who hath laid down his armor,
When the sword hath finished his victory,
Letteth his soul forth as a young eagle
In every morn, with the sun upon its wings,
And the rose kiss of morn upon his chest,
Unfettered of the day,
Freed for the heights.[12]

By the time Pearl Curran died on December 6, 1937, she had pended 4,375 pages from Patience Worth!

Not only has great literature come directly through spirit, but also great music and art. Rosemary Brown has been in contact with composer Franz Liszt since she was seven. As a adult, she has channeled new compositions of the famed composer of the *Hungarian Rhapsodies*. Mrs. Brown also claims to be in contact with Frederic Chopin, Ludwig Von Beethoven, Edward Grieg, Claude Debussy, Johannes Brahms, and Franz Schubert. They come to visit this modest English woman to dictate new compositions and give their messages as well. Chopin had this to say: "True music, real music, great music, is something that is beyond your world, and springs from the spiritual aspects of man; the realization of the greatness and the oneness with God. Great music is something really born in the spirit and is reproduced perhaps very badly, in your world."

The world's greatest artists have also come through to continue their art. In Brazil, medium Luis Gasparetto reports artists of the likes of Picasso, Degas, Van Gogh, and Monet continue to paint though him. The medium works quickly in a light trance completing his paintings in a matter of minutes. Many of his works of art bear styles reminiscent of deceased painters. What is even more amazing is that Gasparetto does these paintings in a darkened room, often painting the picture upside down! Along with Ruth Montgomery's books, the Seth books became popular in the 1970s and 1980s. Their author, Jane Roberts, began receiving messages from an entity known as Seth, after she wrote a book on ESP in 1963. Seth gave this gave this advice to spiritual seekers: "You create your own reality. You form your experience according to your thoughts, emotions, and beliefs. Whatever you focus on in your mind will be materialized in your life. If you want to change your reality, you must first change the thoughts and emotions that you focus upon. Roberts went on to write several books channeled by Seth in including, *The Nature of Personal Reality*. Jane Roberts left the world all too soon in 1984 after a long bout with cancer.

In the 1980s, a more flamboyant trance channeler appeared on the scene—J. Z. Knight. Knight first saw her guide, Ramtha, when she playfully put a model of a pyramid on her head. Ramtha appeared with these words: "Beloved woman, I am Ramtha, the Enlightened One and I have come to help you over the ditch." For next seven years, Ramtha, a 35,000-year-old spirit warrior prepared her as his channel. J. Z. Knight later opened Ramtha's School for Enlightenment. According to Ramtha's teachings on the brain, the primitive mid-brain is wired for intuitive and spiritual experience and through consciousness and energy training, people can become their own spiritual masters. Ramtha attracts many followers such as actress Linda Evans who have popularized his teaching.

While Ramtha is an incarnation of the a 35,000-year-old warrier, Lazaris has never been in earthly incarnation. His teaching reflects less the warrior spirit and more the compassionate soul. Jach Purschel met his guide while meditating on October 3, 1974. Lazaris said his name and gave Jach the message, "Keep moving, keep moving." Jach with the help of his wife, Penni, began giving workshops and started making audio and video tapes of sessions in 1985. When I first met Lazaris in 1990, I was initially skeptical. At the close of the meditation session for 500 people at the Boston Sheraton Hotel, Lazaris gave five messages—one of which was for me. Lazaris said, "To the lady in the corner with her hands clasped tightly over her solar plexus, "Remember, nothing changes until you do." I knew then Lazaris was genuine. There was no way a man with his eyes closed in a dark room could see "a woman with her hands clasped tightly over her solar plexus" forty feet away, let alone bring in a personal message with so much love!

I am sorry that I never had a full reading with Lazaris—his energy is just delightful. However, I have had a yearly reading with trance channeler Elwood Babbitt every year from 1980 until a year before his death in 2000. Babbitt first became known in the field though his biography, *Voices in Spirit*, written by Harvard Professor Charles Hapgood. Elwood was also tested favorably for astral travel at the American Society for Psychic Research in New York City. His real claim to fame was his trance mediumship, which transformed the plain-spoken farmer into the erudite Dr. Fisher. While in trance, Dr. Fisher would quickly correct the sitter, when he was addressed as "Elwood" by intoning with his impeccable English accent, "I am Dr. Fischer."

Elwood Babbitt lived modestly while on the earth plane, content to live out his last years in a small rented home in Cabot, Vermont, with his last wife, Daria. He loved to have fun. Even in his seventies he would roller-skate with his teenage daughter, Anya, and he enjoyed playing his favorites on a juke-box which took up half the kitchen! His real legacy was his books—*Talks with Christ and his Teachers, The God Within: A Testament of Vishnu*, and his last channeled book, *Perfect Health*, reportedly channeled by Wilhelm Reich and Rudolf Steiner. Other personalities who came through included Albert Einstein, Mahatma Ghandi, and Mark Twain, as well as less-known figures such as Jim Cole. When Charles Hapgood asked Babbitt to contact the Hindu deity, known as Vishnu, part of the spiritual trinity Brahma, Vishnu, and Siva, he didn't realize what a strain it would be on the medium's health. Exposed to such high, intense energy, Elwood Babbitt became ill for several weeks. Finally his main guide, Dr. Frederick Fischer, managed to buffer the high frequencies so Babbitt could continue. The book contains transcripts of sessions from July 19, 1970, to December 6, 1972. Professor Hapgood asked the force many questions, including one on how to deal a "brother in error."

CHARLES: "To maintain the balance in our own life, when we find a brother in error, what shall we do?"

VISHNU: "When we are coerced, when we are ground down to the gross earth, when we are used as a mere instrument, when we are hurt by the unjustifiable attitudes of a selfish being—then the words ring out loud and clear across the heaven: it is your duty if you be true upon this pathway, to turn the other cheek and to give only an expression of love to those who would hurt you and deny your birth right."[13]

The book brings to light some interesting occult history. When asked about Joan of Arc, the Vishnu Force explained she was gifted spiritually, receiving voices of the masters, which only she understood. As for Mary Baker Eddy, the founder of the Christian Science religion, she was reported to have been a medium. When asked if Levi's, *The Aquarian Gospel of Jesus Christ* was correct, the Vishnu praised the book as "a text of excellency for all those who seek a truer understanding." As for the principles of psychology formulated by Dr. Sigmund Freud, "they do not enter a deep enough understanding to accomplish their purpose."

Throughout the dialogues, the Vishnu master force talks of the "spiritual positive" and the importance of thought vibration. Vishnu concluded the dialogues with this reminder to spiritual seekers: "Remember well whatever you reflect into the world, you are speaking as a god to a god."

Daniel Douglas Homes (1833-1886). Courtesy of Prints and Photographs Division, Library of Congress.

And as you express to one another the fullness of your love, then you grow into a fullness of *your* compassion, where you see the magnitude of Eternity, and see that there is nothing impossible, but only all that is possible when the true balance of your life if combined with full spiritual knowledge and understanding."[14]

Many who received readings from Elwood Babbitt subscribed to these high ideals of compassion and spiritual truth. Often we were told to maintain a positive thought vibration and prepare for more difficult times ahead. Dr. Fischer made many predictions of coming earth changes which would effect the West Coast first. He urged people to prepare by being more self sufficient, to stockpile a year's supply of food and water, and encouraging moves to rural areas of upper Maine and Vermont. Elwood himself took Doctor Fischer's advice, moving first to upper Maine and later settling in Cabot, Vermont, where he passed into higher life in 2000.

Margery Crandon. The last of the great physical mediums. Courtesy of PrairieGhosts.com.

Chapter Four:
Esoteric Anatomy, Auras, and Table Tipping

"Before we can transcend limitations, whether in our own nature or in the circumstances around us, we must try to understand what it is that they are meant to teach."

—N. Sri Ram

In order to understand how physical mediumship works, a through knowledge of esoteric anatomy is needed. All cultures have recognized an inner energy system. The Egyptians called it "ka," the Chinese, "chi," the Japanese "ki," and the Hindus "kosha." *Ka, chi, ki,* and *kosha* are all names for the energy which surrounds the physical body.

In addition to the etheric double, we have an astral body, essential for the dream state. When we fall into sleep, the astral body detaches safely from the physical and moves about the universe. For those able to obtain a deep dream state, astral travel is ever possible. Authors such as Robert Monroe and William Bulhman have detailed their books on the out of body experience.

The fourth body is termed the mental body, and it is the bridge between the three lower bodies—physical, etheric double, and astral body; and the three higher bodies—the higher mind or manas, the Buddhic body, and the Atmic body. As Edgar Cayce, the Sleeping Prophet, stated, "Mind is the builder." The last three bodies form the soul and stay with us, carrying a permanent record.

The fifth body is related to clairaudience. Then the sixth body is our individual portion of the Divine called the Buddhic body. This body is related to spiritual vision and clairvoyance. The seventh body is called the Atomic body and it is important in channeling and trance mediumship. Professional physical mediumship develops in stages. While some fortunate souls come into the world with the gift, most, like any talented artist, have to hone their skills. The first stage then of physical mediumship is opening the third eye. It is important to see spirit in order to gain a strong connection with guides. Almost everyone in the field has at least five guides—a personal guide, a doctor of chemistry, a doctor of philosophy, a joy guide, and an American Indian for protection.

A sequence of inner development may begin with intuition as the fourth charka expands. Many fine detectives and psychologists go by gut feeling. This is the opening of the third charka in solar plexus. Later, as the fourth charka expands, there is a greater knowing or inspiration. Many artists, poets, and writers experience this when they are engrossed in their work

Psychic gifts are observed when the three upper charka are open. When the fifth charka opens, clairaudience, or the voice of spirit, is heard in the inner ear. It frequently sounds like someone is calling your name through a tunnel, as spirit forms an astral tube to amplify the sound. Many times, people turn around when someone clearly calls their name, only to see no one there. Other times, clairaudience sounds like static radio transmission. However, with concentration, the sound can be tuned in.

Next, the third eye or sixth charka will open naturally with meditation and spiritual guidance. During the initial stages of opening the third eye, the student will see tiny pin points of white or blue lights about the size of a dime. Later, other colors may appear or larger lights. At this point, don't be surprised if you see an outline of spirit called an aura. Usually, the aura is about a few inches above the ears and goes in a semi-circle shoulder to shoulder. In the final stage of clairvoyance, spirit can be seen as clearly as a materialized form. Great clairvoyants, such as C. W. Leadbeater, have even peered clairvoyantly into the atom before microscopes. When science was able to look inside the atom, there was the same structure that C. W. Leadbeater had drawn many years before in his book, *Occult Chemistry.*

Once the third eye is opened, then the next stage is to deepen trance. A deep trance allows the connection between guides and the physical body of the medium. Without this connection, the energy needed to move a trumpet, or for spirit to draw or speak would not be present. However, it all begins with mental mediumship—clairvoyance, clairaudience, clairsentience. In mental mediumship the medium connects with spirit through the third eye (sixth charka), clairaudience, (fifth charka) and clairsentience (the fourth chakra) While the medium hears with the inner ear, it is only in clairvoyance, that the medium sees the spirit.

There are several time-honored methods of opening up the third eye. One is to align the seven bodies through meditation. When this is done, the meditator makes a direct connection with his/her guides. According to the Tibetans, who are masters of the art of meditation, the lay person is advised to observe The Five Precepts. For a monk there are 227 monastic rules. These five rules are an excellent way to begin the path of mediumship as well:

1. I undertake to abstain from harming living beings.
2. I undertake to abstain from taking what is not given.
3. I undertake to abstain from sexual misconduct.
4. I undertake to abstain from false speech.
5. I undertake to abstain from intoxicating drugs or drink.

The Tibetan Book of Mental Development advises first year monks:

1. "Enthusiastic perseverance should be like a stream, study and practice without break."
2. Citing laziness and forgetfulness as obstacles to meditation, the Tibetan guidebook advises a quiet place, full instructions before retreating, and a meditation teacher to guide the student.
3. Mental agitation, excessive sensuality, and negative spirits (living and dead) should be avoided if the student wishes to progress on the spiritual path.

What actually happens in meditation? As the physical body becomes more relaxed, the astral body can detach. In the astral body, the meditator is now freed to make contact with loved ones, guides, and angels. With sincerity and effort, the meditator may journey to higher planes—the higher mental plane, the Buddhic plane. In deep meditation, a state of trance is entered. Often, the meditator experiences inner awareness and peace. The ultimate goal of meditation is Nirvana—cosmic consciousness.

A regular time and place for your inward journey. Then, begin with a prayer of protection or simply surround yourself with white light. The yogis use a meditation cushion or rug to buffer themselves against unwanted earthly influences lingering on the ground.

Candle Meditation

Meditation is the first step in opening the third eye. In addition to inner peace, it helps to build up the aura and add protection to your life force. Over a period of regular practice, meditation can help develop the gifts of telepathy, clairvoyance, and mediumship. The key to all meditation is regular practice.

One of the best exercises is the candle meditation. Set aside twenty minutes a day at the same time and place to practice this exercise. Start by sitting in a straight-back chair in a comfortable position with feet on the floor. Place a candle on a table opposite you at eye level, about three feet away. Gaze at the candle for a minute. When you close your eyes, you should see an image or small dot. Follow this afterimage in your mind's eye. Try to hold the image as long as you can. If the image floats away from your gaze, concentrate on bringing it back. Gradually lengthen your meditation time from five to twenty minutes.

With patience and regular practice, students report telepathy, clairvoyance, and mediumship experiences after a period of about ninety days. I am partial to the candle meditation as it was one of the first techniques I utilized to open my third eye. Basically, I would practice every afternoon. At first, it was just the inner image of a red flame that bordered the blue. Later, the flame shifted into shapes or symbols. About the sixth week, the flame became a portal to the other side. I saw many spirits crowding in. Since I had read in an Edgar Cayce book that this was a lower phase of mediumship, I ignored the crowd and sought a higher plane. Soon, I came in contact with a man who had lost his legs. He seems to know me and said he was related to me. Next to him was a kind, slender lady holding a purple flower. She spoke: "This is my name."

The next time I saw my mother, I asked her, "Did we ever have any relative who lost both of their legs. "Yes," Momma answered, "My grandfather—Grampa Brickett had diabetes and lost both his legs a year before he died. He had a housekeeper named Violet who took care of him." I knew then that I truly was reaching the other side in meditation. For those who wish to develop their mediumship, working with a professional medium is a big help. Sitting in a circle on a weekly basis will bring out your psychic gifts though intention and meditation plus spiritual guides. I know. I "sat" in Reverend Gladys Custance's circle on Friday nights for three years before I was certified as a Spiritualist medium. The training I received in meditation, mediumship, and psychometry was invaluable.

Often students who first see clairvoyantly will ask me, "How do you know that you are seeing with your third eye. "Just close your eyes," I advise. "If you still see the lights with your eyes closed then it is true clairvoyance." Many students have their first clairvoyant experience when they see an aura. I shall never forget the first time that I saw an aura. It was at the Park Street Church in Boston. Reverend Gladys Custance was sitting next to me as we listened to Harmon Bro, author of several books on Edgar Cayce. As Reverend Bro stood in front of the pulpit, delivering his speech, I saw a golden yellow light about twelve inches radiating from shoulder to shoulder. I nudged Gladys, "Is Harmon Bro's aura yellow?" Gladys nodded, "Yes."

Gladys had seen many auras in her day. I once asked if there was ever a time when she had not seen an aura? "Only once," she said. Apparently an elderly lady had taken a long bus from her home to the First Spiritualist Church in Onset, Massachusetts. When she sat down for a reading, all Gladys could see was a black shade being pulled down. Not wanting to upset her, Gladys made an excuse that she wasn't well enough to do a reading that day. However, her perception was quite accurate as the woman died within the week.

Like Gladys, I have seen my share of auras, so few events surprise me. However, voices and sounds that occur in the background of my readings always fascinate me. More than a few times voices can be heard in the background, saying, "She (referring to the medium) can't hear us" or "Wait until she is ready." Once, I even picked up a heart beat of a spirit. When an acquaintance, Sharon, passed over, her husband Randy came for a reading. I wanted very much to make contact with her, but since I already knew her by sight, a physical description of her spirit would serve as little evidence. The reading went well and Randy left satisfied. Later that night he phoned—as he had played the tape back, when Sharon was talking, her heart beat could be heard. Even when the tape was turned over the heart beat continued until her spirit finished talking. Apparently Sharon "knew" my concern and came in loud and strong!

A more common experience is to see an aura around the individual. Analysis of size as well as color and texture can reveal much. For example, I was watching the *Johnny Carson Show* one late night, when he introduced the writer of Peter, Paul, and Mary's new hit single, "I'm Leaving On a Jet Plane." A boyish John Denver was coaxed on stage. Immediately upon seeing how wide his aura was, I sensed he would be a big star quite soon. The same was true when a stylish Russian lady came for a reading with her niece to interpret. Before the woman had her coat off, I remarked to her niece, "Your aunt must be very well known—she has quite large aura." "She is a very famous opera singer in Russia!" her surprised niece replied. The wider the aura, the more influence a person has. If an aura is very close to the body, this can also indicate ill health.

Next, color is important. Red shows vitality; however, too much red can reveal anger and rage. Frequently, red is strong in the auras of athletes. Orange indicates pride and is a good money-making color. Successful people from sales to the performing arts have some orange in their aura. If you believe in yourself, others will too! However, too much orange may indicate false pride or stubborn qualities. Next yellow is the color of the mind. Teachers, for example, may have yellow in their auras. Pale yellow can show a timid nature, but a bright yellow indicates confidence and a sense of humor. Green comes next and is the middle color of the color spectrum. It is the color of harmony and denotes compassion. Doctors, nurses, and social workers have a lot green in their auras, as do mothers of young children. Blue indicate a spiritual quality, ranging from blue-green which likes to help in a practical way to true blue, the color of an idealist, to the deep cobalt blue of a psychic. Ministers, as well as mediums, have blue in their energy fields. Purple is the last color and is rarely seen in most auras. It is a color of deep devotion. Edgar Cayce felt purple indicated change, and once the decision was made, the purple would settle into blue.

Combinations of colors are also important. Many police and firemen have the blue of service combined with red, indicating a preference for physical activity. Deep kelly green combined with cobalt blue may indicate a spiritual or psychic healer. Sometimes combinations can indicate ill health. One client walked in my office with an aura half black and half purple. I could clairvoyantly see a priest behind her trying to help her—hence the purple of devotions, but on the other side was a deeply negative entity. I urged her to seek psychiatric help as she was deeply depressed. Unfortunately, within the week she was admitted into Hartford Hospital with an diagnosis of schizophrenia.

Sometimes colors in the aura change over time. One regular client came in with a vastly changed aura—the same colors but now pastel in shade. It turns out, she had been diagnosed with M. S., a progressive disease sapping her strength. Often, the opposite is true: a client with gray in their aura may return after a few sessions with vibrant greens and blues, indicating spiritual acceptance of their issues of life and a change of consciousness. Of course, it is these positive changes that make the job of a psychic so gratifying.

At the New England School of Metaphysics we teach a course entitled "Auras." Students just love to see auras. To help them view an aura, we have one person stand against a white wall. Then the other students concentrate on a spot about twelve inches above the head. With practice, a light or aura will be detected. Next, the subject is asked to think of a guru or a saint. The aura expands. Conversely, the aura retracts, if the person is asked to recall a sad experience in life.

Another course that is a favorite with students is "Table Tipping." In the Victorian era, the idea of assembling a group of people around a table to communicate became commonplace—even fashionable. Queen Victoria, Mary Todd Lincoln, and Harriet Beecher Stowe all believed in spirit communication. Table-tipping was the rage in Victorian, and later, Edwardian times. Why not? Modern spiritualism began with the physical phenomena of spirit raps; table tipping made an appearance as well. Soon, home circles began across the country. It peaked during World War I as people wished to communicate with their dead relatives.

No wonder. The technique is simple. All you need is a table, preferably a round wooden table. Start with a small light table (even a card table will do). The table should be wood, a natural conductor of energy. Avoid press wood or particle board, as it does not conduct the energy in a natural pattern, thereby impeding transmission. At the New England School of Metaphysics we have had good luck with a three-legged, round, antique mahogany wine table.

Whatever table you choose, it is very important to cleanse it before you use it. This is easily accomplished by placing the table under a full Moon or spraying it with a light mist of sea salt and water and wiping it dry to clear the energy. Next, dedicate your table to spiritual service by surrounding it with white light. Before you start, say a prayer and call on your angels for additional protection. Some people like to keep an open Bible in the room as well.

Once your table is properly cleansed and dedicated to spiritual service, you are ready to start. Assemble a group of spiritually-minded people to practice table tipping. It is important that there is no skeptic in the group as this can lower the vibration. The group can range from two to eight people. Start by having the group place their fingertips lightly on the table. Then, as is done by our Table Tipping Class, sing songs to bring the energy up. (Since I tend to sing out of tune, I enlist one of our better singers to lead us in songs such as, "You are my Sunshine" or " I've Been Working on the Railroad.") Soon, the sitters begin to feel like their fingers are tingly and melding in with table. At this point, vibrations are felt, going across the table. This is an exciting experience for beginners.

At this point, I will sent up a code. If the table goes toward me, this indicates a "yes" answer. If the table moves in the opposite direction, this indicates "no." Soon, spirit is fielding questions, to the great delight of the students. For example, one participant asked, "Will I be taking a trip to New Hampshire?" The table indicated, "No," and sure enough, the trip was cancelled.

While the group is having fun posing questions, it is also important to keep a record of the session. If not, important information is lost, and to be honest, spirit gets miffed if we are sloppy in our methods! A good practice is to have a tape recorder running. Be sure to start with date and time, the names of those present. Then describe weather conditions or temperature in the room. Take a moment to tape any observations such as, "Now the table is vibrating" or "We can all feel a chill in the room."

Charles Webster Leadbeater (1854-1934). Courtesy of the Theosophical Society in America.

Once the table is vibrating, the next step is to get the table moving so that is up on two legs and thumping with the third leg. The guides informed me before our table tipping class began that this would take about three practice sessions. Sure enough, on the third try, the antique wine table was rocking on two legs.

This time we established a code: one knock for "yes," and two for "no." After working this way, we asked sprit to give us his name by tapping out the alphabet. The first letter was an "E," then an "L." We needed to go no farther. I knew the spirit well—Elwood Babbitt!

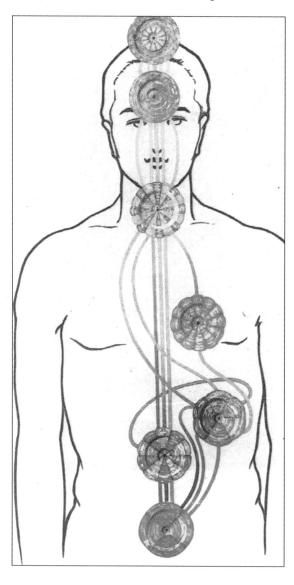

Charles Webster Leadbeater's diagram of the chakras. Courtesy of the Theosophical Society in America.

Chapter Five:
Psychic Photography

"People only see what they are prepared to see."

—Ralph Waldo Emerson

The most convincing evidence of physical mediumship is a photograph. If a picture is worth a thousand words, a psychic photograph is worth a million! Nothing is more convincing to the skeptic's eye than a photo of a spirit casually sitting by a tree or ascending a staircase. Of course, some may still disbelieve, blaming the quality of the film or integrity of the photographer. Unfortunately, too few photographers possess this rare talent—and those who do, are often ridiculed for their efforts.

Such was the case with William Howard Mumler, a Boston engraver (1832-1884). Mumler, no stranger to the Spiritualist movement, was married to Hannah Mumler, who claimed the ability to see spirits. In fact, she would often describe the spirit before the image appeared to the photographic plate. Spirit raps and other manifestations, such as Mumler's camera "dancing" or vibrating would be observed in the studio.[1]

Mumler's psychic photography began in 1861, when an extra figure of his cousin, who had died twelve years before, appeared on a photographic plate, much to his surprise.[2] Soon, spirits were spotted on other photographic plates when Mumler was present in the room—sometimes, even when he was not the photographer. Many ordinary people, as well as the leading Spiritualists of day, such as Emma Britten Hardinge, flocked to his Boston studio at 285 Washington Street. Mrs. Britten, the noted actress turned medium, was overjoyed to see the spirit of Beethoven standing behind her in her photograph taken by William Mumler.[3] When the Honorable Moses Dow, editor of Boston's *Waverly Magazine* came in for a photo, he was pleased to find the spirit of his deceased assistant editor, Mabel Warren (page 68).

William Mumler's most famous patron was Mary Todd Lincoln. She was an ardent believer in spirit communication, as were other notables of her day, such as Queen Victoria. Mrs. Lincoln even invited medium Nettie Colburnn Maynard to the White House for a séance after the death of their son, Willie, in 1862. After President Lincoln's assassination, his widow sought solace from many sources, including William Mumler. Using the alias of Mrs. Tyndall, Mrs. Lincoln sat for a photograph. When Mary Todd Lincoln sat for a photograph with Mumler, she was quite pleased with the results. The image of her deceased husband appeared when the plate was developed. Both she and the surprised photographer immediately recognized the figure of Abraham Lincoln that appeared over her shoulder in the photograph. The American Museum of Photography has the picture on their website. Here the shadowy, but distinct, figure of President Lincoln is seen standing lovingly behind his wife.

Not all of Mumler's patrons were as pleased with their photos. In 1869, Mumler was arrested for public fraud. Some claimed these photos to be that of deceased relatives, while other said the "spirits" were living people. In fact, the Prosecution was able to show that a so called "spirit" was in fact the image of living human being. The case held in New York City attracted national attention and a full cover page in *Harper's Weekly*. In the end, the case was thrown out of court. However, though the expensive trial put a damper on William Mumler's career, it did not end it. Still professing his abilities, Mumler later published a pamphlet on spirit photographs and even advertised, in 1875, the ability to take images of person not dead, but at another location.

Unfortunately, all the secrets died with William Mumler, as he requested that all negatives be destroyed following his death in 1884. However, the sheer volume of supporters led credence to his work: According to one researcher, a Mr. Glendinning, the

Mumler case settled the question of psychic photography. "Had there been no other proof, this sworn evidence of scientific men, bankers, and merchants, lawyers, photographers, and others at the Mumler trial was overwhelmingly abundant."[5]

In England, more psychic photographs emerged. The first were those of the spirit of Katie King, materialized with the help of medium Florence Cook. Cook (1856 – 1904) became known for her full materializations of her controls—a child, Katie King. Cook was so secure in her abilities, that she invited reporters from the *Daily Telegraph* on October 10, 1872. Later, a reporter saw faces during a séance and on August 12, 1873, the reporter was able to take a picture of Katie King!

Scientist Sir William Crookes investigated Cook's work with very favorable results. Crookes reports in the *Spiritualist* dated April 1874, noting: "Katie never appeared to greater perfection and for nearly two hours she walked around the room, conversing familiarly with those present." During the séance the spirit of Katie King sat on the lap of a sitter who felt a light-weight child, and at another, she allowed a sitter to cut a piece of her dress.

The next famous psychic photographer was William Hope, born in Crewe, England in 1983. He inadvertently discovered an extra image of someone not physically present in a photo. That image turned out to be a deceased sister of the person in the photo. Soon, a group of six people organized a Spiritualist circle for Hope, which became famous, known as the Crew Circle. Later, Archbishop Thomas Colley, an enthusiastic supporter, joined the group.

It wasn't long before others clamored to see Hope's photos—including psychic researcher Harry Price. Price tested William Hope under strict conditions, insisting that Hope use only the photographic plates provided. While this is a good research policy, it is not the best for psychic work, as often the psychic needs to energize the film or plate to get the best result. Price claimed that somehow Hope had managed to switch the "fast" plates he had given Hope for "slow" ones which were of a different thickness, weight, and color. This, of course, led Price to deduce trickery. Others like Reverend Charles Tweedale of Yorkshire stood by Hope's work.

Reverend Tweedale pointed out that even people who called on Hope "unannounced, even with secret identities, they still obtained clearly recognizable spirit images."[7]

These conflicting reports on William Hope's work left many questions. While some believed the spirit photographs to be genuine, others felt his work lacked authenticity. Certainly, some psychic photos, such as those of the fairies taken by young girls in the 1920s, turned out to be admitted fakes. Others, however, deserve to be taken seriously. It seems that, at one time, physical phenomena was so often faked that some Spiritualist camps, such as the Lily Dale assembly, voted to ban all physical mediumship—a rule that is still enforced today.

In terms of authenticity, one psychic photographer of the last century stands out—Edward Wyllie. Unlike spirit photographers—William Mumler and William Hope—Edward Wyllie was never accused of fraud. Before he became noted as a psychic photographer, Wyllie had earned his living as a cartoonist, an auctioneer, and a soldier. According to Fred Gettings, author of *Ghosts in Photographs*, "Few psychic photographers have had as many remarkable testimonials and recognitions from their sitters as the American Edward Wyllie.

Like Mumler, who began to hate the "self-appointed investigators," Wyllie was also studied by many experts, and even by a few psychic societies, who all eventually attested to his ability to provide spirit photographs under test conditions.[8] Others who praised Wyllie's work included Dr. H. A. Reid and Reverend Cook, as well as Scottish researcher James Coates. In 1909, Coates sent a lock of his wife's hair to Wyllie in Los Angeles. Wyllie used the lock of hair as a stimulus to obtain a spirit picture of Mrs. Coates' grandmother.[9]

The spirit photographs were meticulous in their details. Frequently, "extras" would appear in Wyllie's photographs, such as the image that appeared in the picture of Mr. Robert Whiteford (page 69). Another interesting "extra" appeared in the photograph of an eighty-eight-year-old Californian gentleman, John R. Mercer. Both his mother and first wife, Rachel, who had died many years before, appeared in the photograph. Closer scrutiny of the picture revealed that Rachel was holding flowers identical to those held by John Mercer's second wife, Elizabeth, before her burial. According to researcher Fred Gettings: "The important point about this picture is that, even though the lower face does suggest that it was based on a process image, probably a screened print, the likeness itself, which Mercer attested to, could not have been derived in such a way, as she had been buried for sixty-nine years, and no daguerreotype, painting, or screened block could have been made of her during her lifetime!"[10]

Not all spirit photographs are taken by professional mediums; some professional photographers have captured spirit on film as well. One of the best examples of this is the ghost of Rayham Hall taken by photographers hired by Lady Townsend to photograph her home in England. Mr. Shira was just setting up his equipment, when he spied "a vaporous shape that gradually took the form of a woman wearing shroud" moving down the spacious staircase. The spirit captured on film is thought to be the ghost of Lady Dorothy Walpole (1686-1726,) who'd resided in Raynham Hall. In real life, she had lived a cloistered life in the home following a love affair.

Besides historic homes, cemeteries have been known to attract paranormal activity: Jude Huff-Felz, of the Ghost Research Society in Bachelor's Grove Cemetery, Chicago, Illinois, snapped a picture of a woman with long hair and bangs sitting on a tombstone. Could she have been one of the mourners of day or a victim of one of Chicago's gangsters when the cemetery was used as a dump site for gangsters?[11]

While most amateur psychic photographers do not get full figures such as seen in this photo, images of orbs and mists abound. Can they be faked? Of course. However, for those who are sincere about capturing spirits on film, here are some suggestions from the experts. First it is important to gain rapport with spirit. Ask permission from your loved ones and guides. Chesterfield medium Robert Channey even suggested connecting with the energy of the film though meditation and prayer. The same could be said for gaining rapport with the camera as well. Channey who worked 1940s, 50s, and 60s, used photographic paper, which he placed against his solar plexus in mediation. When he developed the film, an image would appear often of a spirit guide or departed loved one.

Enid Hoffman gives this version of Solar Plexus Photography in her book *Develop Your Psychic Skills*. After each person is given a three-by-five inch piece of photographic paper, they are seated in a circle in a dark room. Participants are given these instructions:

> The participants must first relax and center, entering a non-mind state, and then clearly visualize the picture each desires. When this visualization is clearly formulated, including elements of personal feeling and meaning, it is ready to "photograph." When ready each participant should press the slick side of the paper against his or her solar plexus, maintaining clear focus of the picture for about ten minutes. All must be silent so there will be no distraction. At the end of ten minutes, collect the exposed pieces of paper and seal them in the protective envelope again. Then take the pieces of paper to a person or firm who will develop them.[12]

Enid Hoffman also suggests trying this exercise with a Polaroid camera. This time, visualize the picture on your "third eye" in the middle of your forehead. Concentrate in the same manner. After a few minutes, have the photographer place the Polaroid camera about an inch from the forehead and snap the picture. As with any new skill, patient practice brings the best results. Sometimes, an electromagnetic field meter (EMF meter) can be of assistance. Once a hot spot has been located, it is important to take a photograph immediately. Also during séances, often orbs, mists, and even the full outline or body of a spirit will appear. Position a photographer opposite the medium to capture flashes or light that occurs during the séance. Be patient. Remember also to be clear in your intention, and ask spirit permission before you enter their realm. And don't forget to surround yourself with white light and a prayer for protection. Often fledging mediums see orbs of light fly across the room during a séance or circle. Always begin with a prayer for protection such as, "We call that which is for the highest good of each and ask that their loved ones, guides, and angels be present."

Then a glass of water is placed beside each sitter, or if you prefer, under each seat. Water is basically used as a conductor for ectoplasm. *Note*: use a glass rather than a paper cup, as the glass will hold a charge of energy better than paper. Allow sufficient time for the medium to gain rapport. Then with the medium's permission, take a picture. Simply let the medium point spirits out for you during the séance.

Any camera will do. Some prefer a digital as it eliminates any criticism of flaws in the film. As for film, some psychic photographers swear by infra-red, others prefer Kodak 400 Gold, or 200 speed film. What ever method you choose, if the conditions are right, orbs will crop up in photos. These orbs can vary from a few inches to several feet in diameter. With practice, larger orbs appear. Sometime even a full face will appear with distinct features of the deceased spirit in the center of the orb. Whether in the form of orbs, mists, outline, or full figures, spirits are there in full force during séances and Spiritualist circles.

Ghosts can also be found in historical homes. When I was doing psychic photography for *Connecticut Ghosts*, I visited the homes of Theodate Pope Riddell, William Gillette, and Mark Twain. Their presences were felt. All three homes seemed alive with energy. By combining mediumship with an EMF meter, and a Kodak "throw away" camera, I was able to capture mists and orbs quite readily. In fact, the spirits seemed to enjoy visitors!

Spirits also like to be part of experiments. This was the case with Robin and Sandra Foy, and Alan and Diana Bennett, who formed a group in England known as the Scole Group. "They put brand new film on the table which had never been in a camera Afterwards the films were developed. Images were found on them, handwriting, hieroglyphs, and other symbols and messages."[13]

The group, which began early in 1993, continued to meet on a regular basis, and by October 1995, senior members of the Society for Psychical Research began to observe, test, and record what they termed the *Scole Experiment*. The S. P. R. verified that handwriting and images appeared on unopened, factory-sealed photographic film. The messages appeared in different languages, such as Sanskrit verse, which was later translated into English: "Whatever work is done here in this life for the satisfaction for the mission of the Lord is called bhakti-yoga or transcendal loving service to the Lord and what is called knowledge becomes a concomitant factor.[13] Among the images they received was a clear portrait of Sir Arthur Conan Doyle, an image of Saint Paul's Cathedral, an image of the Seine River taken from Notre Dame Cathedral, as well as a photograph of the *Daily Mirror,* Dec 16, 1936. Dr. Ernst Senkowski, an experimental physicist, concluded, "My observations, as well as later personal reports of my colleagues, left me convinced of the genuineness of the phenomena."

"Moses Dow with the Spirit of Mabel Waren." Photogrpaher, Willliam Mumle. B. Becker Collection/American Museum of Photography.

Mr. Robert Whiteford with an "extra." Photographer Edward Wylie. B. Becker Collection/American Museum of Photography.

Chapter Six:
Electronic
Voice Phenomena

"What happens after death is so unspeakably glorious that our imaginations and our feelings do not suffice to form even an approximate conception of it."

—Carl Jung

Not only do spirits enjoy being seen, they love to be heard as well. Researchers report that John Belushi's ghost uttered, "Hidden Morphine." Marilyn Monroe's spirit playfully inquired, "Do you want to see a movie?"

Are these messages received by electronic voice recording (EVP) investigators real?

"Yes," according to Tom and Lisa Butler, directors of the American Association for Electronic Voice Phenomena. Hundreds of their members report receiving similar voices from loved ones through EVP. Many of their members have become interested in EVP because of a loss of a child or an interest in metaphysics.

Lisa Butler, initially, became interested in EVP through her study of metaphysics. While attending a seminar on psychic development at the Delphi University in 1995, she had an amazing experience. As she tells the story: "The voice of Arthur Ford (a deceased medium) gave me three messages. The first was a personal message for me. The second prediction stated that Tom and I would be running an organization that would help others learn that death was not the end. The last message was to tell Patricia (Patricia Hayes, the director of Delphi University) to get some cards."[1] Sure enough, the personal message was accurate; and further more, Patricia Haynes did need business cards. Later, Lisa and Tom became the directors of the American Association for Electronic Voice Phenomena as "Arthur" had prophesized. It would also have been characteristic of Arthur Ford, a medium famous for his Houdini Séance and the first televised séance (which was conducted for Bishop James Pike), to be interested in EVP. After all, he was as well known for his clairaudience, as he was for his trance mediumship.

While hearing and recording voices was new to Lisa Butler, the idea has been around for a while. Thomas Edison, in fact, believed communication with the other side was possible: "If our personality survives, then it is strictly logical or scientific to assume that it retains memory, intellect, other faculties, and knowledge that we require on this earth. Therefore, if personality exists after what we call death, it is reasonable to conclude that those who left the earth would like to communicate with those they have left here."[2]

The World Broadcasting Company (now Decca Records) was also intrigued with the idea. On April 23, 1933, they set up a test to see if researchers could communicate with the spirit world. Paranormal researcher Hereward Carrington attended, as did Helen Bigelow. Several voices from the other side were recorded. One simply announced: "Surviving personalities speaking to you from another dimension."[3]

Since the World Broadcasting Company preferred to keep the event quiet, Friederich Jugernson knew nothing about EVP when he placed his microphone on the windowsill to record the songs of wild birds in his country home in Sweden. In June of 1959, Jugenson became the father of modern EVP. When he replayed his to reel tape recorder, he heard white noise or a "roaring, hissing static sound." What a happened next was EVP history. He heard a male voice saying something about "bird songs at night."

Jurgenson was quite surprised to say the least as he noted: "My first thought was the tubes were damaged during travel. Nevertheless, I turned the recorder on again and let the tape run. My second recording was just like before: I was hearing this strange hissing and the distant bird chirping. Then all of a sudden there sounded a trumpet solo as if to announce something. I listened with continued surprise as suddenly a male voice began to speak Norwegian. Though it was very quiet, I could clearly understand the words. The man was talking about 'bird songs at night' and I heard a number of chattering, whistling, and splashing sounds and among them what seemed to be the chirping of a sparrow."[4] Jugenson, who heard thousands of these voices, published a book on his experiences *Voice Transmission with the Deceased*, which was followed by *Voices From the Universe*, and *Radio Link with the Beyond*.

Latvian researcher Dr. Konstine Raudive was inspired by Jugenson to do some research of his own. While Jurgenson simply recorded air, Dr. Raudive devised his own methods: "Often he taped radio static, obnoxious hissing rasp between stations. Like Jugenson he countered the possibility that he had recorded breakthrough radio broadcasts by pointing out that the voices spoke to him by name. And many, he said, spoke Latvian, even though Raudive resided in Germany."[5] Many of the messages were profound such as this one from the spirit Adolf Homes: "All your daily events your thoughts and actions as well as events you seem unable to control such as environmental catastrophes, in the final analysis, were created by yourself, though they originate in other dimensions, in dreams and in other trance-like conditions when you were your real self."[6] Apparently we also have free will, and according to the spirit of Adolf Homes, death is one of many possibilities open to us. Dr. Raudive chronicled 72,000 "voice texts," many of which appear in his book, *Breakthrough*.

In the United Stated, EVP was researched by George Meek in 1971. When Meek was introduced to a medium and electronic engineer Bill O'Neil, unusual things began to happen. They made contact with the spirit of Doc Nick who supplied the technical information needed to communicate. They dubbed the device spiritcom. Soon, another spirit joined the team. Dr. Mueller obligingly supplied information about himself—his profession as a college professor, and his social security number, both of which checked out. Mueller also liked to talk shop:

> Mueller: "By the way, did you get the multifaceted crystal?"

> O'Neil: "No, I got the five faceted one from Edmund's."

> Mueller: "Edmunds? Who is Edmunds?"

O'Neil: "Edmunds is a company. Edmunds Scientific."

Mueller: "Oh, I see. Well, very good."[7]

George Meek was so excited about spiritcom that he even held a press conference on April 6, 1982, at the National Press Club. Unfortunately, few reporters attended.

In Europe, Han-Otto Koenig, an electronic engineer, did work similar to Meek and O'Neil, when he set up a device for live spirit broadcasts in Luxenborg. The audience was amazed to hear a voice from the other side say: "Otto Koenig makes wireless with the dead." Two mothers even verified that they heard the voices to be those of their of their deceased children.

Perhaps the most touching aspect of EVP, are the communications from spirit children. Many EVP researchers in Italy, Brazil, and the United States have found this to be so. Many children's voices were heard through "Electro Acoustic Voices" developed by Marcello Bacci of Grosseto, Italy. Bacci, a paranormal enthusiast since 1949, began recording voices using an old vacuum tube radio. Scientists were astounded at Bacci's results. Professor Maro Salvatroe Festa, who had studied Bacci for six years describes EVP sessions. "A typical session begins when Bacci turns out the lights and tunes the radio to white noise. Everyone waits patiently until Bacci announces he hears the voices. Then Bacci asks: 'Friends, we are here. Can you make yourself heard?' Only then are the voices heard by others in the room. When children from the other side communicate with their parents, joyful and very emotional reunions take place."[8]

The same scenario held true for Brazilian Sonia Rinaldi in 2001, when she began to use EVP to help parents communicate with their "dead' children. When parents make an appointment with Rinaldi, they are asked to submit ten questions. At the appointed time, Rinaldi is on one phone with the parents, while another is directly connected to her computer for EVP. The results are nothing short of amazing. For example, here is an EVP transcript received by Luis and Virginia, two medical doctors who lost both their daughters—Lucianne and Viviane—in a tragic automobile accident in November 2001. One year later, they made contact with their deceased daughters:

Luiz: "How are you there in the spiritual plane?"

Young girl: "It is proper peace."

Young girl: "I will call you up."

Luiz: "Are you both together?"

Young girl: "You called us here and I heard you."[9]

In the United States, many parent have also received EVP messages from children in spirit. One grief-stricken mother, Martha Copland, wrote a book, *I Am Still Here* on the subject. Her daughter, Catherine, who died in a car accident December 23, 2001, gave the EVP message which became the title of the book—"I am still here." Cathy is continuing to help others. She is part of a group on the other side called the *Big Circle* which helps other deceased children communicate through EVP.

When human contacts make up the vast number of EVPs, other dimensions have been known to come though. Sarah Estep, the founder of American Association for Electronic Voice Phenomena (AAEVP) has had such experiences. Sarah first began her research in the 1970s, interested in the paranormal through the Seth books by Jane Roberts. When she heard about the early EVP work of Friederick Jurgenson and Konstantine Raudive, Estep decided to give EVP a try. After experimenting for one week, she received her message in response to the question: "Please tell me what your world is like."

According to Estep, "In several seconds a *Class A* voice replied, 'Beauty I am.'"[10] Later, she made contact with another dimension and with the composer Beethoven. She founded the AAEVP association in 1982, and wrote *Voices of Eternity* which chronicled her journey into EVP.

Just as it is possible to record voices of the dead, so images can also be copied on film. In 1985, Lucas Schreiber invented a device dubbed Vidicom. He was successful in capturing faces of his deceased daughter, Karin and others including actress, Romi

Schneider. His method? "The technique used by Schreiber consisted of aiming a video camera at the television. The output of the camera was then fed back into the television thereby creating a feedback loop."[11]

In 1986, Marty Harsch-Fischbach and Jules Harsch tried their hand at video-taping spirits with some success. Their information came from an EVP guide named Technician. With the aid of Technician and another group of spirits known collectively as the Timestream Research Group, the couple was able to receive clear images of people from the spirit world. One especially poignant contact was from the spirit of Dr. Konstantine Raudive, an early pioneer in EVP. According to researcher Ernest Sankowski: "There is no question that the Harschs are psychic and mediumistic. No doubt that they realized genuine phenomena that could not be faked by any normal means."[12]

Even more amazing phenomena occurred when four friends, Robin and Sandy Foy, and Diane and Alan Bennett got together in Scole, England to try their hand at EVP. They contacted a guide named Manu. They were richly rewarded with EVP recordings, which included an audible performance of Rachmanioff's *Second Concerto*. They also received over fifty apports (materialized objects) which included solid objects, such as coins and jewelry.[13] The group known as the Scole Group has been favorably researched by the Society for Psychical Research based in London. In addition to the apports, the spirits gave specific instructions on communication devices designed to talk to the other side: "The (spirit) team had asked them to provide a simple battery-powered tape recorder from which the microphone had been removed. After a few crackles and whispers, a whispered voice said 'Hello' through the amplifier."[14]

The spirit team insisted that they were utilizing or stretching energy and the team gave complex instructions for building communication. Instead of utilizing ectoplasm to build a voice box through which the spirit could speak, "the spirit team said the new energy would be used to generate 'energy voices' which could address the group from midair."[15]

This took a bit of time. The first try was not successful, but the second communicator, White Cloud, was audible to all present: "White Cloud was obviously a very powerful guide. His voice was quickly audible to all. However, he told the group that he had tried to speak to them many times before in the circle, but none of them had heard him because the frequency of vibrations had always been wrong for this type of communication."[16]

While I have never had the pleasure of working with the Scole Group, I did attend a seminar given by Tom and Lisa—two very dedicated professionals—in the company of eleven other participants. Some of the participants at the EVP workshop at Omega Holistic Institute in New York came from as far away as Haiti. I brought with me my standard Radio Shack tape recorder and placed it in the middle of our group circle. When I asked for a message, I received these words: "Protect _____ Anthony," which were clearly hard by the group when Tom Butler put the tape through the amplifier. Anthony is my husband's late father. We had recently been given the same message through Reverend Hoyt Robinette, that Anthony was protecting our teenaged son, Michael. My seminar partner, Sandy, received a message from her grandfather, and several other participants had EVP messages from loved ones.

I was also fortunate to attend an EVP seminar with Reverends Brian and Lynn Kent. These two Spiritualist ministers used an IC recorder and a hair dryer for the "white noise" which spirit needs to produce sound. "Basically," Reverend Brian Kent suggested, "just turn on your tape recorder, along with the hair dryer for about five minutes. Interact with spirit by asking questions. 'Who is here?' 'Do you have any messages?' Then wind down by stating, 'We are going to end the session; do you have anything else to say?' Wait a minute and then shut the recorder off."

The Kents have recorded hundreds of EVPs with this method. Two of their favorite EVPs are from children related to them in spirit. Lynn who had a miscarriage feels that the spirit of that child came through with this message: "Perry" (Lynn's Maiden name) followed by a child-like voice states slowly, "I … love … you." Brian also received a message he feels came through twins who were stillborn.

On the tape, you came hear giggling, then six clicks followed by the message: "Daddy, Daddy, we are here, we are here."

As the Kents explained, EVP takes some patience to master, but the technique is not particularly difficult. First, you need a tape recorder either a standard cassette recorder or a digital note taker. An IC recorder is preferable. For starters, good choices include IC recorders, Panasonic DR 60, QR 80, QR 100, or QR 200—all models recommended by EVP researchers.

Next, white noise is needed as a means for recording spirit voices. Apparently, the spirits utilize the white noise in order to be heard. Anything from a the sound of water running or a hair dryer blowing, to the hum of a fan in motion, or just plain radio static can be used for white noise. Once you have white noise and a tape recorder in hand, find a location that is filled with spirit energy. This locale could be the home of a deceased relative, a cemetery, or a historical site. Be sure to get permission to tape in the location. Surround yourself with white light and then ask permission from the spirits to record their voices. Mentally, try to communicate as well. Take time to make a list of people you would like to contact. Don't be afraid to ask questions. Wondering if I should pursue EVP, I asked for spirit help. When Reverend Carl Hewitt's voice came through with "Carl" in his familiar Southern drawl, I knew I had made contact. The story doesn't end there. At the same time I heard Carl's voice, I received a message of encouragement mentally: "Keep going. You are close to a breakthrough." Pay close attention to both your thoughts and feelings as you record, and also listen to the EVP tapes.

When it comes to hearing voices on tape, it is necessary to amplify the tapes and to graph the sound visually. In order to do so, Tom Butler was most helpful sharing his technical knowledge. He recommended a sound editor such as Audition or Audacity to amplify, filter, and even reverse sound file. According to Butler, "You can either make the recording on a tape recorder and then play the tape into the computer for review, editing storage, or attach a microphone directly to the computer and use the sound editor as a tape recorder. When transferring into a computer, make sure the computer is set for 'Line In' recording in 'Sound and Multimedia' in the 'Control Panel' of your personal computer. If you must take sound from the 'earphone jack' of your recorder, consider purchasing an 'attenuating cord' to match the difference in resistance between the two jacks. Radio Shack can help."[17]

It was fascinating to see our EVP recording visually graphed on the computer screen. Deftly, Tom would point the spaces that indicated the changes in frequency of an EVP. Usually EVPs can only be heard with amplification. However, not all EVPs are as clearly heard as a *Class A* recording; some are *Class B*, which can only be heard over the speaker with some effort. There may be some disagreement about what is said. *Class C* voices can be heard only with head phones, and even then may be difficult to understand.

Pointers for EVP Sessions

If you want to be a successful researcher:

- Keep notes with dates, locations, times, and feelings that occurred during sessions.
- Label all tapes with date, time, and place.
- Familiarize yourself with the history of the area.
- Tape when your energy is high and you can devote the concentration necessary.
- Always begin your EVP session by asking spirit permission.
- Do not be afraid to test a spirit once you make contact. Ask questions like, "What is your name?" How did you die?" "What was your favorite food?"
- Remember, most of all, that the spirit does have a message for you—if take the time to listen.

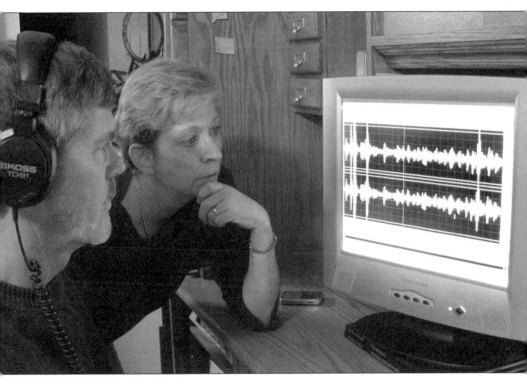

Tom and Lisa Butler, Directors AAEVP. Courtesy of the
American Association for Electronic Voice Phenomena.

Chapter Seven:
Opening the Third Eye

"Never forget that life can only be nobly inspired and rightly lived if you take it bravely and gallantly, as a splendid adventure in which you are setting out into an unknown country, to meet many a joy, to find many a comrade, to win and lose many a battle."

—Annie Besant

The ancients knew nothing of EVP or psychic photography, yet they were very much in touch with the other side through clairvoyance. I vividly recall a clairvoyant episode that took place when I was five. A Hindu gentleman, only I could see, started giving me instructions from the other side. "Cross your fingers and place them over the middle of your forehead. Now concentrate and push the energy out." Soon I was able to visualize people and see them in their future state. Other guides quickly followed: an Egyptian master and an ancient Chinese doctor.

Sometimes guides come in on an "as needed" basis. Recently, I retired at about ten pm one autumn evening, a bit on edge. My husband and our son were away on a hunting trip. Every sound seemed to echo through the house, from the whirl of cars passing by to the tick of the clock on the night stand. Even the white noise from the heating ducts seemed to be magnified.

To be honest, I wasn't used to being home alone. It was after midnight before I finally fell asleep. When I awoke, at about five am, I saw an Iroquois Indian with a Mohawk-type hair style and a leather quiver across his bare chest. He was as real as any human being could be. As he faded before my surprised eyes, I realized that this brave had come to protect me through the night. Knowing this, I slept soundly the rest of the week. While I was born with a very open third eye, others can develop it through training. There are three avenues to development clairvoyance. One is the a Spiritualist development circle. Just sitting in a circle on a weekly basis will bring out your psychic gifts though intention and the help of spiritual guides. A second method is through the study of dreams—everyone has some psychic ability in the dream state. The third method to open the third eye, universally accepted by East and West, is meditation.

I "sat" in Reverend Gladys Custance's circle on Friday nights for three years before I was certified as a Spiritualist medium. The training I received in meditation, mediumship, psychometry, and clairvoyance was invaluable. Often, the first thing a student will sense is a charge of energy as spirit enters the room. This is called "a change of forces," and is present at the beginning and end of a circle as the spirits enter and leave the room. Next, a cool breath or pressure on the head and back of the neck may be felt. Sometimes the energy will become charged with light, fragrance, or a hum—all signs that spirit is in the room. Often, clairvoyance begins with seeing tiny spirit lights. Students sometimes wonder whether it is poor eye sight or spirit lights. "Just close your eyes," I advise them, "If you still see the lights with your eyes closed then it is clairvoyance." Colored lights, like the aura, need some interpretation. White light, in many circles, is Christ light or the most perfect energy. Red light is for vitality. Orange, a sacred color in the East, may indicate a Hindu presence or positive energy. Yellow and gold light give powerful energy of knowledge and attainment. Green light is often used for healing, especially physical healing and balance. Blue light is the light of spirit—cobalt blue helps to open the third eye. Finally, violet light is for spiritual healing and transformation.

Often the whole circle will experience these waves of color. At this point, the group is ready for the next step: seeing the shadowy outlines of guides and loved ones. Frequently, the medium will point to different students and ask, "Can you see any spirits in the room?" or "Have you any messages from spirit?" The mature student will then give out whatever impression he or she has been given, and mentally ask for more information such as a name or the relationship of spirit to the group. Frequently, by tuning in, student mediums sense the height, color of hair, and clothing of the spirit. Later, a good clairvoyant will see this in vivid detail. Some professional mediums, such as English spirit artist, Coral Polge, and her American counterpart, Reverend Rita Berkowitz can draw the spirits they see with their third eyes.

Clairvoyance takes two forms—objective and subjective. My own development as a medium began with objective clairvoyance. For many years, I believed this objective view of spirit as the only form of clairvoyance. When I began to sit in a mediumship development circle, I soon saw pictures of spirit in my mind's eye (subjective clairvoyance). At first, I distrusted these impressions. Little by little, I began to describe the spirits seen inwardly to others in the group and soon realized subjective clairvoyance is as valid as objective clairvoyance. In fact, sometimes it is an easier method for spirit to communicate, as physical manifestation takes a lot of energy on the part of spirit.

There are pros and cons to both forms of clairvoyance. In Spiritualist circles, subjective clairvoyance seems to be more common. This may be because objective clairvoyance cannot be developed by will alone, as spirits do have some control and can decide if they wish to manifest. While seeing spirit is rare for adults, many children from ages two to seven have mystical experiences in the form of imaginary playmates. Often these children objectively see spirit until adults tell them it is their imagination! Of course, some adults do retain their clairvoyance. Several, such as Alice Bailey, Charles Webster Leadbeater, and Geoffrey Hodson come to mind. All these natural clairvoyants chronicled their adventures in books. Alice Bailey, who initially protested she had little time for channeling, eventually agreed to take dictation from her spirit Tibetan guide, Djwhal Khul. She channeled twenty-four books on subjects such as *Esoteric Psychology* and *Esoteric Healing*. Charles Webster Leadbeater and Geophrey Hodson were prolific writers as well. Leadbeater, author of *Occult Chemistry*, had the ability to see inside an atom before microscopes were able to penetrate its structure. His books *Clairvoyance, Charkas*, and *Man Visible and Invisible* delineate the color and structures of the charkas and auric field. Geoffrey Hodson, clairvoyantly verified much of Leadbeater's work, and added his own clairvoyant analysis of the auras of the developing child, material which makes for fascinating reading.

Later, in the 1970s, another Theosophist, Douglas Baker, wrote a text on clairvoyance entitled *Opening the Third Eye*. Baker was so ardent in his desire to serve humanity that he became a medical doctor so he could legally diagnose with clairvoyance. Among the techniques that Dr. Baker recommends is candle meditation—discussed at the end of this chapter. In order to open the third eye, Dr. Baker advised that the seeker perform service to mankind, study of ancient wisdom, meditate, and live a life based spiritual principles. The spiritual aspirant, according to Baker, "cannot expect to confine his activities to a brief half-hour each day or an hour a week or merely attend a lecture somewhere. He is struggling towards a psycho synthesis—the assembling of the personality around a higher point of vibration—and must give himself every chance to proceed smoothly."

Sometimes people develop clairvoyance through careful study, while others spontaneously become clairvoyant through trauma or near-death experiences. Such was the case for Damion Brinkley who was struck by lightening while talking to a friend on the telephone during a thunderstorm. Brinkley was hit so severely that the nails in his shoes were glued to the floor. He survived to write about his 1975 near-death experience in *Saved By the Light*. While he was being resuscitated, he found himself in a crystal cave, attended by *Beings of Light* who gave him a glimpse of the future—including a cowboy with the initials R. R. who would become president in 1980. At the time, Brinkley thought that Robert Redford would be elected—not Ronald Reagan! He was also told by these the *Beings of Light* that he had a mission left on earth. When he came back to life, he did so with the ability to read minds and to predict the future himself.

Although Damion Brinkley met his guides while on the brink of life and death, most people meet guides in meditation, dreams, and visions. Contacting guides is the first step to mediumship, for remember, "Like attracts like." The masters only serve those who serve others with compassion. And angels are said to come only to those who have a pure heart! A medium is assigned guides based on the individual's consciousness as well. Almost everyone in the field has at least five guides—a personal guide, a doctor of chemistry, a doctor of philosophy, a joy guide, and a Native Indian for protection. Sometimes, guides show up suddenly. This was the case for artist Glenda Greene when the Master Jesus appeared before her. She began to receive regular visits and was able to paint a portrait of the Master. She wrote of her experiences in *World Without End*. Jesus left her with sage advice on many aspects of life. For example, Jesus explained about problem solving:

> To solve a problem, it is first necessary to view it from a higher level. This is especially easy to observe in the area of physical healing. A physician or any medical facility can only arrest an illness, keep it from progressing, or reduce infection, thus providing conditions in which healing may occur. The actuality of healing is always a miracle that happens on a higher level through the restoration of wholeness. No matter what the problem, healing always comes from a higher level.[3]

However, not everyone has access to a trained clairvoyant or medium to facilitate opening the third eye. While a development circle led by an experienced medium is the safest and fastest way to develop clairvoyance, there are other methods such as dream analysis and meditation. Almost everyone is psychic in dreams, so by recording dreams, one can meet guides and loved ones. Paul Twitchell even received philosophy that he called Ekcankar through dreams. Twitchell recorded his 1957 spiritual experience in his book, *The Tiger's Fang*. Seven years later, he became a "Mahanta" (a great soul) though inner initiation.

Dreams may be spiritual communication as in the case of Paul Twitchell, or purely physical in origin. More often dreams can be the result of a salami sandwich chased down with two cups of coffee and blueberry pie than a meeting with God. In order to interpret dreams, the dreamer's level of consciousness—physical, mental, spiritual—must be first determined. While some dreams are indicative of indigestion and anxiety, others, called lucid dreams, have psychological and spiritual communication. Here, one can meet a guide and receive spiritual communications just as the late Paul Twitchell did. All that is needed is a pen and paper to take down the direct communication. Other dreams, which may be just as worthy, need to be deciphered, as the messages are given though symbols. A good dream dictionary such as Kevin Todeschi's *Dream Interpretation (and More) Made Easy* will come in handy.

Colors and Symbols in Dreams

Pay attention to colors in dreams. For instance:

- Red can mean "Stop!" or it could stand for anger.
- Orange is the color of health and vitality, and a sacred color in the East.
- Yellow represents the mind and positive mental energy.
- Green is the middle color of the color spectrum and stands for balance and health.
- Blue is often associated with the sky and inspiration.
- Black can be death or ending.
- White is purity or the medical field.
- Purple, the last color of the spectrum represents change (according to Edgar Cayce). Other psychics see it as a spiritual healing or devotional color.

Just as colors play a role in dreams, symbols are important too. Elsie Sechrist in *Dreams: Your Magic Mirror*, says the face can be symbolic. Hair, for example, may symbolize your thinking—messy hair being confused thoughts. Eyes stand for vision. If you have a patch over one eye, then you are literally seeing things from one eye or one-sided perspective. The mouth represents speech; therefore if a dreamer has loose teeth, he may need to watch his speech!

Beside the study of dreams, meditation offers a sound method of opening the third eye according to author Elsie Sechrist. As a young bride, she consulted with medical clairvoyant, Edgar Cayce, because she was given less than a year to live due to a heart condition. Edgar Cayce not only cured her, but also inspired her to study meditation and dreams. Later, she wrote two books on Edgar Cayce's work: *Dreams: Your Magic Mirror* and *Meditation: Gateway to Light.*

Cayce's approach to meditation emphasized that ideals should be established: "Ideals are set from spiritual purposes, spiritual aspirations, desires, and there is a pattern in Him who is the way, the truth, and the light, and when that pattern is set according to such judgments, we find there is never the condemning of another. Because others do not agree with thee, condemn them not. For that what judgment is mete is measured to thee again."[4] Once the ideal is established, mental and spiritual preparation and patience are needed. While it may be difficult to be patient, it is an active process—one which can redirect and refine the soul.

Meditation is then the key to opening the higher centers for creativity, clairvoyance, and healing. Alice Bailey, who channeled *Discipleship in the New Age*, gave meditation instructions for both individuals and groups who wish to progress. Her guide, known as "the Tibetan," advised his students to put aside time for a structured mediation: "I am going to ask you to give two relatively brief periods of time each day to a definite and defined meditation. One period, (the most important) must be given to general group mediation, and the other to that meditation which I feel will enable you to function as an integrated personality, fused and blended in the consciousness of the soul."[5] Thus, with loving service (group meditation) and spiritual integration (personal meditation) much progress can be made on the spiritual path. The Tibetan master gave this meditation for groups:

The Great Invocation
> From the point of Light within the Mind of God
> Let light stream forth into the minds of men.
> Let Light descent on Earth.
>
> From the point of Love within the Heart of God
> Let love stream forth into the hearts of men.
> May Christ return to Earth.

From the cntre where the Will of God is known
Let purpose guide the little wills of men--
The purpose which the Masters know and serve.

From the centre which we call the race of men
Let the Plan of Love and Light work out
And may it seal the door where evil dwells.

Let Light and Love and Power restore the Plan on Earth.

For anyone meditating in a group or alone, the process is the same: Sit or lie down in a position that allows for a straight spine. Then focus all attention on one point whether it be music, a mantra, or even the breath. As the brain begins to relax as it gently slips from beta waves to alpha waves and with more practice deeper delta waves. Meditation not only changes the brain waves of the body, but it also can affect the vital functions of the body such as blood pressure and temperature.

Researchers such as Dr. Gregg Bradden, believe spiritual practices like meditation can even change DNA; while others such as Dr. Herbert Benson recommend meditation to lower blood pressure and prevent hypertension. Dr. Benson even observed Tibetan monks able to withstand freezing temperatures while meditating all night in light robes without apparent discomfort. Instead of frost on their robes, a light steam appeared!

In the East, there are also several methods to develop meditation. One that has recently come to the attention of the Westerners is *The Tibetan Book of Mental Development,* based on Tibetan Buddhism. In this classic text, first year monks are taught, "Enthusiastic perseverance should be like stream, study and practice without break."[6] Citing laziness and forgetfulness as obstacles to meditation, the Tibetan guidebook advises a quiet place, full instructions before retreating, and a meditation teacher to guide the student. Mental agitation, excessive sensuality, and negative spirits living and dead should be avoided if the student wishes to progress on the spiritual path.[7]

What actually happens in meditation? As the physical body becomes more relaxed, the astral body can detach. In the astral body, the meditator is now free to make contact with loved ones, guides, and angels. With sincerity and effort, the meditator may journey to higher planes—the higher mental plane, the Buddhic plane, and finally Nirvana or cosmic consciousness.

It is important to set aside a regular time and place for your inward journey. Then, begin with a prayer of protection such as The Lord's Prayer or simply surround yourself with white light. The yogis use a meditation cushion or rug to buffer themselves against unwanted earthly influences lingering on the ground. Then begin the practice of meditation which can be listening to music, gazing at a candle flame, or listening to the voice of the silence.

Katherine and
Harry Brickett.

Sketch of Harry Brickett. Drawn by Spirit Artist: Reverend Rita Berkowitz.

Chapter Eight:
Trance Mediumship

Say not, "I have found the path of the soul." Say rather, "I have met the soul walking upon my path."

—Kahlil Gibran, The Prophet

There are many exceptional trance mediums. Some, like Edgar Cayce, Madame Helena Blavatsky, and Andrew Jackson Davis are very well known. Their work is kept alive by the groups they left behind—Edgar Cayce, the Association for Research and Enlightenment, Madame Blavatsky, the theosophical movement, and Reverend Davis, the Spiritualist church. Others, like Elwood Babbitt, Paul Solomon, and Gordon Michael Scallion are known only to a few. Many, such as Alice Bailey and Jane Roberts, were genuinely surprised by their gifts.

When Jane Roberts made contact with Seth, she said it was "as if someone had slipped a cube of LSD in my drink." Alice Bailey even argued with her guide, the Tibetan master, Djwal Khul, that she had three girls to look after and little time to take down his dictation. Of course, she did find time, and went on to scribe twenty-four books. She, like Jane Roberts, channeled for circles of thirty or so students, while modern channelers, J. Z. Knight and Jack Burek channelled before audiences filled with hundreds of well-heeled customers with additional profits made in book and tape sales. Whether rich or struggling, famous or nearly famous, these mediums have one thing in common—they are all full-trance mediums.

These mediums, by the way, do not look like their Hollywood prototypes. Jane Roberts, slender with mousy-blond hair and glasses could easily pass for a librarian, while glamorous J. Z.

Knight could pass as movie star Linda Evans' twin sister. In fact, the majority of the trance mediums I have known are the least likely people in the room to be identified as psychics. Reverend Gladys Custance, for example, looked like your grandmother, a slightly round gray-haired lady. Elwood Babbitt, on the other hand, dressed like a rugged farmer in blue jeans and a plaid flannel shirt, with a mug of coffee in one hand and a cigarette in the other. In contrast, Gordon Michael Scallion was neatly attired in a button-down shirt and dress pants, looking more like a computer salesman than a futurist, especially when he arrived with audio equipment and over-sized speakers ready to tape his lecture at Asnuntuck Community College in the early 90s.

Of the these trance mediums, I knew Reverend Gladys Custance best. Not only did I study with her for three years, but we remained friends for over twenty-five more. During that period, I had many opportunities to observe her remarkable channeling.When she channeled her guide, a Hindu she dubbed Professor, it truly was like being in the presence of royalty. It was really Professor who did the readings and instructed the class though the entranced Reverend Custance. Professor was so much involved in her mediumship that at one point in her development, Gladys explained: "Professor would not let me read any books as he did not wish me to be influenced by outside sources."

I first met Gladys Custance after a service at the First Spiritualist Church of Onset one hot evening in August 1969. She and her husband, Reverend Kenneth Custance, were still grieving the death of Meroe Morse who had been like a daughter to them. The childless couple took Meroe's death in the Spring of 1969 pretty hard. Meroe, along with Jean Crown, were young people that Gladys and Kenneth had groomed for mediumship as teenagers.

Both Jean and Meroe had turned out to be amazing mediums. In fact, Jean wrote in Chinese calligraphy as a four year old. Her father, a medical doctor, brought the sheet of paper with Jean's calligraphy into a colleague at Harvard. The professor identified the calligraphy as ancient Chinese writing! Later, Jean moved to Somerville, Massachusetts, just outside Boston and became one of the city's busiest mediums.

Meroe was the more materially successful of the two protégés as a graduate of Wellesley, majoring in art, who went to work for Polaroid in the 1950s. Soon, she became one of the company's executives with several copyrights to her name. She was also a talented clairvoyant and quite close to Gladys, who always wished for a picture of Professor to show others. Gladys's request was granted when Meroe Morse, both an artist and a clairvoyant, was sleeping over. Professor appeared at the foot of her bed quite early in the morning. Excited, Meroe telepathically asked for permission to sketch the spirit guide. "Certainly," he answered and stayed for about an hour. When Kenneth saw the likeness, he requested a picture of his guide, a Franciscan monk termed the Abbott. A few months later, the brown-robed monk appeared to Meroe for a sitting. Both are reproduced on page 102.

For many years, Reverend Gladys Custance was the only trance medium I knew. It wasn't until 1980, that I met a second trance medium—Elwood Babbitt. His first reading for me floored me and left me scurrying to the library to look for places with exotic names, such as Machu Picchi and Qumran. Dr. Fischer, Babbitt's guide, had said I had lived in Machu Pichi and had been a scribe in Quonram. He also told me something I had known for several years, yet had never revealed. This was that my father had been a famous Roman Emperor in a past life. Even though I had seen this clearly in a dream, I chose to keep the information to myself. When Dr. Fischer said, "Your father was once known as Tiberius in his Roman life, you could have knocked me over with a feather! I was so intrigued by Elwood's trance reading that I scheduled one a year for over twenty years.

It was quite fitting that Jon Klimo sets the scene for his book, *Channeling*, with a description of Elwood Babbitt entering trance: "In the trance session (Elwood) Babbitt, sitting upright in a straight-backed chair, appears gradually to fall into a deep sleep. This "sleep" is sometimes brief, sometimes prolonged. Changes in breathing occur and the expressions of his face also change. After a while there are movements of the lips and other muscles of his face that suggest the efforts of the incoming entity to gain control of them. Finally the entity greets the sitter and starts to talk…"[1]

Often, the entity would announce, "This is Dr. Fisher taking control of the body." However, others guides came through, such as Mark Twain, Jim Cole, Albert Einstein, Mahatma Ghandi, Rudolph Steiner, Royal Rife, psychiatrist Wilhelm Reich, and Edgar Cayce. Several of the guides even channeled books—*Talks with Christ The Testament of the Vishnu* and *Perfect Health*.

Few people have witnessed trance mediumship on the level demonstrated by Elwood Babbitt. Trance mediumship occurs in levels from light control, when the medium is overshadowed, to full-trance mediumship as with Elwood Babbitt or Edgar Cayce in which the spirit completely takes over the physical body and consciousness of the medium for the purposes of spirit communication. In a light trance state, the mediums do have some memory of the session, while in deep-trance there is no recollection of the trance communication. Physical changes are present as well as mental ones. For example: slowing of the heart rate, deep rhythmic breathing, lowered body temperature, and reduced or no reaction to pain and touch. Edgar Cayce went into such a deep state of trance that investigators were able to remove a toe nail without any discomfort to the Sleeping Prophet. However when he awoke, Cayce was in such pain that he vowed never to submit to any more researchers!

Edgar Cayce also exhibited a change in consciousness, beliefs, and even speech patterns—frequently diagnosing in the language of a old-time doctor. Often his sentences were filled with repetition, reversal of sentence structure, and language and grammar from the 1800s. The same was true for Jane Roberts and Eileen Garret when their guides came through in trance. Robert's guide, Seth, waxed philosophical during her channeling sessions with a cadence and speech pattern completely different from the medium. Eileen Garrett's channeling was even more sophisticated as she channeled four entities, all with distinct voice patterns, inflection, and consciousness!

While scientists may not believe in trance mediumship, they are able to shed some light onto what actually happens in trance by measuring brain waves. Science has found that there are varying levels of consciousness from a waking Beta state to a light hypnotic trance of Alpha to a deep trance state of Theta to an unconscious Delta state:

Beta—(13+ cycles per second) waking state, active consciousness, affirmations.

Alpha—(8 to 12 cycles per second) daydreaming, meditation, light trance, light hypnosis.

Theta—(5 to 7 cycles per second) deep trance, deep hypnosis, deep trance

Delta—(5 to 4 cycles per second) Unconscious (For those who are trained to maintain consciousness lucid dreaming and astral travel).

The mind never really ceases to function, but only varies in levels of consciousness. When a medium is in the most unconscious (Delta), he or she is said to be in "dead trance" that is needed for full-trance channelling, trumpet mediumship, and spirit art. Full trance mediumship relates to the seventh chakra which is opened for spirit to take direct control of the medium. In lighter states of trance, other aspects of mediumship are seem. As the student consciously opens each chakra for mediumship, development occurs along these lines: Full trance seventh chaka Clairvoyance, sixth chaka Clairaudience, fifth chaka Inspiration, fourth chaka Clairscience, third chaka. (See Glossary.)

Many attune to spirit through clairscienece or a gut feeling—the kind you get when you just know who is on the other end of the telephone. Inspiration is more common with artists, writers, and musicians. After all, the creative process is one of mystery. However, direct communication with spirit through clairaudience, clairvoyance, and full-trance mediumship takes many years to safely develop.

I had been a clairvoyant for about twenty-five years before I developed as a trance medium. In order to develop trance mediumship, one has to "sit" with another more evolved medium in a circle. My own trance development took place over a period of about four years. During that period, I "sat" to three Spiritualist teachers: Dr. Lauren Thibideau, a registered medium at Lily Dale,

Muriel Tenant, a tutor at the Arthur Findlay College in England, and Reverend Patricia Kennedy, a Camp Chesterfield medium.

My first experience with trance training was at Lily Dale Assembly in August 2002. I signed up for two workshops, "Astral Travel" with Reverend Carol Gasper and "Let's Get Physical" with Dr. Lauren Thibodeau. Reverend Gasper's class began to the tune of "I'll Be Your Angel," by Celine Dion. She included powerful astral travel exercises. She also emphasized the importance of protection, surrounding ourselves with white light, and calling on our guides to be present.

I could feel a strong connection with my teacher, Reverend Gladys Custance, who was now on the other side of life. Her trance had been so natural—she would effortlessly slip into trance while the members of the Friday night circle sang "Divine Love" to the strains of the tune for "Silent Night."

Yes, I thought, as we started the first astral travel exercise, *Gladys is definitely here*. This hypnosis exercise was a guided imagery trip to the other side to meet our guides. It turned out to be the high point of the weekend, when I clearly looked into the gentle eyes of Saint Francis! I also had another powerful experience as I connected with the medium from the other side. I heard distinctly, "Robert," and I knew immediately it was Robert Chaney, the well-known trance medium. Three years later, I was to meet one of his pupils, Reverend Patricia Kennedy in Chesterfield, Indiana.

The next day August, August 14, 2002, my husband, Ron, and five friends went to Dr. Lauren Thibodeau's "Let's Get Physical" class for those who wished to develop trance mediumship. Two of us, myself and Ceil, were already professional psychics; the rest were students. We all listened with rapt attentions as Reverend Thibodeau explained the stages of her own development from simple intuition of following her "gut" feeling to full trance mediumship. It wasn't an easy road. She constantly seconded-guessed herself. As Dr. Thibodeau commented, "No one surrenders consciousness without an argument." I think we all breathed a collective sigh of relief. Trust is a big factor in trance mediumship.

But trust we did, and spirits came through. The highly-charged energy of Assembly Hall made a perfect séance room. Before the end of the two-day workshop, everyone channeled spirit. I channeled an angel by the name of Azul, while student Nancy, channeled another angel, Ariel. She and I both were later to become Integrative Energy masters, a technique which was developed by the angel, Ariel! Ceil gave a dramatic channeled talk by a Babalonian princess to everyone's delight. Our friend, Stanley, channeled an American Indian, which he would also channel the next year at the Arthur Findlay College in England.

Others in our group channeled as well. Maureen channeled Jerry, Vinnie channled Zoe; and my husband, Ron, channeled John. The workshop was special as I felt the presence of Reverend Arthur Ford. He had been a guiding presence in my mediumship ever since he came to me in 1997, with the words: "Houdini has a message for you." On the advice of the spirit of Arthur Ford, I accepted the invitation to be the medium for the Official Houdini Séance held at the Goodspeede Opera House in Haddam, Connecticut that year. When I mentioned Arthur Ford's presence to Reverend Thibodeau, she surprised me by saying that she also felt Reverend Ford's presence, especially in her home. She had purchased his old cottage on 4 Library Street in Lily Dale.

The following June, Ron and I, along with our friends Stanley and Mary Ellen, flew to England to take trance training at the Arthur Findlay College in Stanstead. It was the first trip abroad for the four of us and excitement ran high. We were placed in classes with different tutors. Ron and Stanley had Maureen Murnam as their guide and I was assigned Muriel Tenat, a veteran British medium. She had became interested in psychic phenomena when she purchased a dress shop in the 1960s which turned out to be haunted. She studied mediumship at the Arthur Findlay College and became one of their finest tutors. Under her fashionably attired exterior, Muriel was a crack clairvoyant. Just how perceptive I was to discover, when she tuned into the Reiki symbols I was sending out during a clairvoyant exercise in her "Journey of Trance" class.

With about fifteen in attendance, she placed four in the front of the room with instruction to allow their guides to come through while the other students tuned in clairvoyantly. Many of us were already certified mediums, wishing to become full trance mediums.

In the next exercise, I allowed spirit in and she was pleased. At first, not sure of the process, I began to project Reiki symbols which she picked up immediately. "Elaine," she intoned in her measured British accent, "Are you doing some kind of energy work: I'm getting the squiggly symbols." "Yes," I sheepishly admitted. "They are my Reiki symbols. "No, no, no," Muriel said hastily. "You don't project. Allow spirit to come to you." As the class progressed, Muriel drew the energy patterns she saw around each one. When she came to me, she saw six circles of energy around me which coincided with the sixth charka—that of clairvoyance which is my main talent. She also gave personal attention to posture: "Hold your head up high. Spirit needs room on your neck to form an etheric voice box."

Since this was the first time I had heard about an etheric voice box, I later asked her to explain. "Well," Muriel began, "spirit used ectoplasm to form a voice box under your chin so their voice could be heard—it is quite common." Soon, I was browsing the books at the Psychic News Bookstore around the corner. Here I picked up a copy of *On the Side of Angels*, the biography of Gordon Higginson who had been a tutor at the Arthur Findlay College. Not only was Higginson one of Britain's best known trance mediums, he had the ability to materialize loved ones in the séance room!

When I returned from England, I was very much a believer in physical phenomena, but unable to find such mediums in the United States. When I mentioned this to Reverend Gail Hicks, another Spiritualist medium, she suggested that I go to Camp Chesterfield in Indiana. "They do trance and trumpet mediumship there. Go see Pat Kennedy and Susie Greer—they are the best," she enthusiastically advised in her down-home Georgian accent. Soon I was making the trek to Chesterfield.

My first impression of Camp Chesterfield was like stepping back into the 1940s with quaint cottages and a slower pace. The grounds were an adventure in themselves. One of the first classes I attended, "Meditation," was held in Hett Auditorium, which houses a collection of portraits precipitated by mediums Elizabeth and Mary Bangs in the late 1800s and early 1900s. With all this spiritual energy, it would be impossible not to be inspired to meditate!

I also was drawn to our instructor, Reverend Patricia Kennedy, who had the organization skills of an Air Force officer (she had been for many years), the sense of humor of a Barnum and Bailey clown, (she is, in fact, a graduate of Clown College), and the dedication of a saint (a title she would deny, but deserves!). Later, I later learned she was also a fan of Paramahansa Yogananda and had attended classes in the Self Realization Meditation. Reverend Kennedy is not only a trance and trumpet medium, but a numerologist as well. She presented many different methods of meditation and helped us tune into our guides.

When the class ended, I decided to take private lessons in trance with Reverend Kennedy. In July 2005, Ron and I returned with four students Kim, Becky, Mary, and Nancy. Her method of trance training was similar to the Arthur Findlay College. The basic difference was, at Arthur Findlay, we were trained in day light, while Camp Chesterfield mediums preferred total darkness and would only allow a red light to illuminate the room. Reverend Kennedy also suggested students place a glass of water under their chairs as a conduit. "Drink the water after the séance, she also advised, "as it has healing properties." After we meditated a bit, one person was placed in the front with the intention of channeling spirit, while the other five observed. who went into trance with meditation and deep breathing. While the trance student took her time connecting with spirit, the rest of the class sent energy. Reverend Kennedy continued to give us pointers. Again, we were told, "Hold your head erect so there is a place for spirit to form a voice box." Also, "Have faith in your guides." She spoke directly to each spirit that was channeled asking for a name and other information to gain rapport.

What was it like to go into trance? At first I felt light-headed. Then there was pressure on my head as spirit seemed to come closer, and I felt some buzzing in my ears. Finally, it seemed as if spirit reached in and literally took over my vocal cords. Not wishing to jeopardize the process, I remained still with my head erect—ready for whatever ectoplasm might form around my throat. Before long, I found myself listening to the voice of a male spirit coming from my mouth. All six of us channeled to our immense satisfaction. Some just a few words, others for ten or fifteen minutes.

Trance, by the way, is not an unfamiliar state to me. When I am working as a medium, I start with breathing, down to achieving a light trance. Often, I begin with prayer: "Loving Father-Divine Mother, we ask for that which is the highest and best to come through the reading. We call now on loved ones, spirit guides, and angels to be present with us know amen." Then I do three slow head rolls, followed by seven breaths.

Recently, I have begun to teach trance classes at the New England School of Metaphysics. When students come for instruction, I have them sort out their feelings about trance and their goals. I advice them to be especially clear about what they wish to achieve from trance. For example, do you wish to develop a connection with a spirit doctor for medical clairvoyance like Edgar Cayce or to connect with the Great White Brotherhood for service to humanity like Elizabeth Clare Prophet? Remember, the clearer the goal, the quickly the connection to spirit will develop.

The class begins with a lecture based on *Opening to Channel* by Sanaya Roman and Duane Packer. Then after the break, we arrange the chairs in a circle, and place a glass of water under each chair. Each student is instructed to sit erect and surround themselves with white light of protection, do some head rolls to loosen up, followed by Yogic deep breathing.

Next, they close their eyes and listen to soothing tones of "The Eternal OM" for about twenty minutes. Once everyone is loosened up with meditation, half of the class sits on the couch in my office, while the other half sits in chairs to observe the "channelers." It isn't long before flashes of light and some ectoplasm are seen in the darkened room. Sometimes we even get some spirit raps. After ten minutes, the observers compare notes with the channeler, then the observers switch places to try their hand at channeling.

It takes a tremendous amount of energy for the guide to connect, but it is worth the effort. A word of caution: "Like attracts like." You cannot indulge in alcohol or marijuana and expect to attract a master force. Most people should at least connect with a loved one or personal guide. For example, Sylvia Browne has a guide named Francine and Arthur Ford's guide was Fletcher. As you raise your vibration, you will attract higher guides. Sometimes you will experience a change of forces as a new guide comes in.

Sometimes even Master teachers and angels will come in to assist. Some guides who come with so much light are called *Beings of Light*. Remember also, "By their fruits shall ye know them," so don't be afraid to test the guidance you receive. Reverend Gladys Custance always said, "A master never commands, never demands." They only come with your permission and seek to help, and cannot interfere with our free will. During Reverend Suzanne Greer's "Introduction to the Séance Room" class at Camp Chesterfield, students were given similar advice. "You are in control, not spirit." Do not be afraid to tell your spirit guide if he or she is too close, or you need help with the process of channeling. It is, after all, a two-way process.

While not everyone will develop the trance ability of Andrew Jackson Davis (1826 to 1910), we can benefit from his guidance. A natural psychic who heard voices early in life, Davis received dictations from Galen, the celebrated Greek physician. In 1845, Davis dictated in trance, over a period of fifteen months, *The Principles of Nature: Her Divine Revelations* and *A Voice To Mankind*. Davis went on to write over thirty books on philosophy, health, and the world beyond which he termed "the summer land."

Edgar Cayce, "the Sleeping Prophet." Courtesy of Association for Research and Enlightenment.

He became widely known as a medical clairvoyant, and later in life he obtained a medical degree to facilitate his work. When he retired to Boston, he spent his last years running a small book store and prescribing herbal remedies to his clientele. Early in Davis's work, Galen came through in a vision to hand Davis a magic staff with these words which would serve any medium well: Behold! Here is the Magic Staff. Under all Circumstances Keep an Even Mind. Take it, Try it, Walk with it, Talk with it, Lean on it, Believe in it. Forever.

Elwood Babbitt, "Premier Channeler." Courtesy of University of Massachusetts.

Professor, Guide of
Reverend Gladys
Custance.

The Abbot, Guide of
Reverend Kenneth
Custance.

Chapter Nine:
On the
Tongues of Angels

"Nothing real can be threatened. Nothing unreal exists. Herein lies the peace of God."
—Jesus Christ, A Course In Miracles

Exactly what do trance mediums see for the future? Channelers Levi Dowling, Edgar Cayce, Paul Solomon, Elwood Babbitt, Gordon Michael Scallion, Annie Kirkwood, and Ronna Herman have all received messages concerning vast changes for humanity. They seem to agree that we are heading for a new age. While the Moon regulates the month and the Sun delineates the year, there is a greater cycle which Plato and the ancient astrologers knew about called the Great Year of 26,000 years. This year is divided into the twelve signs of the zodiac, so approximately every 2,200 years, a new age begins. We are now going from the Age of Pisces to the Age of Aquarius. Astrologer, Frances Sakoian placed the New Age at 2012, which coincides with the date given by the Mayan calendar.

One of the first mentions of this new age of Aquarius in channeled literature is *The Aquarian Gospel of Jesus the Christ*. It was written by Levi H. Dowling (1844 - 1911), an American who lived in Ohio, and born into a religious family—his father was a preacher. At twenty, young Levi served in the United States Army as a chaplain during the Civil War. After the war, he attended Northwestern Christian University in Indiana and began publishing Sunday School literature. He was also a graduate of two medical colleges, and practiced medicine for many years before he retired. At fifty, he began to fulfill a recurring vision as a youth of building a white city, which turned out to be symbolic of his work on the akashic records. From two am to six am, he labored on *The Aquarian Gospel*—literally transcribing gospel from the akashic records.

Published in 1908, *The Aquarian Gospel* sheds light on the hidden years of Jesus from the age of twelve, when he impressed the rabbis with his knowledge, until he began his mission at thirty. According to *The Aquarian Gospel,* Jesus, the Christ, prepared for the task by studying in the great mystery schools of India, Tibet, Persia, Assyria, Greece, and Egypt. The gospel makes the distinction that Jesus was a man who brought through the Christ force. *The Aquarian Gospel* also states that Jesus was immaculately conceived and that reincarnation was an accepted belief in his community. Jesus was, in fact, a way shower for those who wished to end the cycle of rebirths: "You know that all my life was one great drama for the sons of men; a pattern for the sons of men. I lived to show the possibilities of man. What I have done, all men can do, and what I am, all men shall be." (Aquarian Gospel 178: 43, 46)

According to *The Aquarian Gospel* (1908), the Age of Aquarius will arrive soon: "This age will comprehend but little of the works of Purity and Love; but not a word is lost, for in the Book of God's Remembrance a registry is made of every thought and word and deed; And when the world is ready to receive, lo, God will send a messenger to open up the book and copy from its sacred pages all the messages of Purity and Love. Then every man of earth will read the words of life in the language of his native land, and men will see the light. And man again will be at one with God." (Aquarian Gospel 7: 25- 28)

Since Levi Dowling's day, time seems to be speeding up. We may well be heading for the Aquarian Age in record time. What took years to discover, now comes to light quickly with the new technology. For example, both Presidents Franklin Delano Roosevelt and John Fitzgerald Kennedy were able to keep their affairs secret while in the Oval Office. However, Clinton's toying with white house intern, Monica Lewinsky, made the nightly news shortly after the event occurred.

Time is speeding up for a reason. We need to change our consciousness, for time is running out. According to Edgar Cayce,

Elwood Babbitt, Gordon Michael Scallion, Annie Kirkwood, and Ronna Herman, vast earth changes are coming. While positive events such as the Harmonic Convergence in 1987 did a lot to delay and lessen the changes, many will still occur.

According to Edgar Cayce, events such as the building of the Golden Gate Bridge in the 1930s increased the positive energy in the region and averted an earth quake that had been predicted. At the time he made the prediction, Edgar Cayce was relatively unknown. That all changed when Marguerite Bro wrote an article about "the Sleeping Prophet" for *Coronet Magazine*.

Perhaps no channeler has been as prolific as Cayce, who channeled over 14,000 readings—many for clients hundreds of miles away. Not only did Edgar Cayce give medical clairvoyant advice, but he also gave readings on earth changes. In 1941, Cayce's guide warned that the United States would experience vast Earth changes including earthquakes that would destroy the West Coast and New York: "Portions of the now east coast of New York, or New York City itself, will disappear. This will be another generation though. The southern portions of Carolina, Georgia will disappear. This will come first. The waters of the lakes (Great Lakes) will empty into the Gulf (of Mexico) rather than the waterway over which such discussion have been recently made (St. Lawrence Seaway). It would be well if the new waterway were prepared." (Reading 11520-11)

Edgar Cayce felt that Virginia Beach would be safe along with Ohio, Indiana, and Illinois. Cayce also predicted eruptions in tropical areas near the equator, sudden physical changes for Europe, and Japan disappearing "in the twinkling of an eye."

Much of Elwood Babbitt's work also centered on upcoming Earth changes which mirror those predictions of Edgar Cayce. One of the few academics to study channeling, Professor Charles Hapgood, studied the earth change reading of the remarkable clairvoyant, Elwood Babbitt from Orange, Massachusetts. Babbitt's life is chronicled by Professor Charles Hapgood in *Voices of Spirit*. Hapgood and Babbitt went on the collaborate on two more books: *Talks with Christ* and *The God Within: The Testament of Vishnu*.

Elwood Babbitt channeled Jesus in *Talks With Christ*. Christ explains that this is time of transition from the values of the material world and an understanding of the spiritual world. On January 10, 1977, Christ spoke these words that day: "What profiteth a man to own the whole world and to lose his soul? What profited a man to walk in the counsel of the ungodly, to sit in the scorner's seat, to cast judgment upon his neighbor? So it is man sits upon the shadows of his mind and sees not beyond to the fullness of his true expression of life, within the shadows seeks the counsel of all worldliness, the negativity of life in all its material forms, rather than seeing the values of all life lie upon the spiritual sounds of Understanding, Love and True Compassion."[1]

His advice to man today?

Christ: "The instructions I gave enter under one title of all life, one which seems an impossibility at the present stage of your society. It is simply expressed LOVE ONE ANOTHER."[2]

Jesus also came through another scribe, Helen Schucman (1909-1981), a Columbia University professor. She was determined to "find another way." As Schulman explained "The head of my department unexpectedly announced that he was tired of the angry and aggressive feelings our attitudes reflected, and concluded that, 'there must be another way.' As if on cue, I agreed to help him find it. Apparently this course is the other way."[3]

Soon, she was having vivid dreams, and her colleague, Dr. William Thetford (1923-1988), encouraged her to keep a record. On the evening of October 21, 1965, she heard what was to become a familiar voice say, "This is a course in miracles, please take notes." For three years, from 1965 to 1972, Schulman received rapid inner dictation. The result? Three books: a 622-page text, a 478-page workbook, and an 88-page manual for teachers.

According to *A Course In Miracles*, we create our own reality: "Projection makes perception." When we see the world as negative, it is because we are filled with twisted defenses and view ourselves as separate from God. The core of *A Course in Miracles* is love and forgiveness. Two key messages of the course are, "Love is letting go of fear," and "Forgiveness is the key to happiness."

Paul Solomon channeled similar advice on love and tolerance in his messages, along with advice on earth changes. The son of a Baptist preacher, Paul Solomon, led a rebellious, alcoholic-fueled life for many years before he realized his gift through hypnosis. When an amateur hypnotist, named Harry, put Solomon in trance, a voice came that was not Solomon's. "Who are you?" asked the hypnotist. The voice answered: "This is not a spirit. This is not a personality. You are not talking with someone else. You are talking with the rest of your mind." Paul Solomon like Edgar Cayce was channeling The Source.

The Source warned that we "are on the brink of death and destruction." Solomon's guide foresaw economic and climatic changes in New England even before the disasters on the West Coast: "Know as well that the changes first affecting this area (New England) will be concerned with failures of production in food and economy, difficulties in that manner as will develop into hostilities and even riots, not so far from here. Particularly in the areas of New York City, Long Island, and surrounding areas and communities and spreading out as if it were a fan. Then following the more drastic changes in the surface of California first, then New York, Long Island, and the coast of Connecticut and Massachusetts. Find both of these inundated. (Solomon Reading, number 886, 9/14/76 4)

Just after the Gulf War in 1991, The Source warned that the United States should try to reach out to Islamic countries. The Source warned that the recent Gulf War was not the end of war in the Middle East: "Be more trouble in the Middle East. For you will find an Islamic leader emerging, and this will lead to that we have spoken of before, an attack on Israel, which will be a major threat of the use of nuclear arms. The recent war (Gulf War) is a portion of the balance of which we speak, and will be re-encountered." (Solomon Reading 9418 September 1, 1991. [5]) When asked if Saddam Hussein was the Anti-Christ, The Source warned of another more destructive leader on the horizon: "He is an Anti-Christ, but only a minor player. For the Anti-Christ who is the absolute embodiment of darkness will appear. But he will appear as an angel of light, and many among you will be confused, for he will first appear to be a savior in the Middle East. But having gained power and favor he will become then power mad, drunk with power."[6]

The readings also stated that Paul Solomon was indeed the incarnation of Paul the Apostle and that the apostle Peter had also incarnated at this time and that John the Apostle had incarnated as John Peniel. They further state "that it is essential that the work of the three apostles John, Paul and Peter together will establish the New Age."[7] Unfortunately, Paul Solomon died in 1994, and John Peniel has yet to come forward.

The readings did give hope that there would eventually come what was termed "a new Eden" in which mankind would rededicate itself to the Law of One—the unity of all life: 'For without the involvement of the entire universe, or this world, or this level of manifestation, there cannot be the evolvement of a single soul, not an atom of the universe—you are the universe! This is the Law of One. In the understanding of bringing all together, there is the understanding of self." (Solomon Reading Number 42 10/19/72 [8].)

Gordon Michael Scallion, a futurist, has made earth changes his focus, publishing a journal entitled, *Earth Change Report*. Scallion's paranormal abilities developed quite suddenly. Like Cayce, Scallion found himself unable to speak when he was giving a business presentation. During his brief hospitalization, Scallion was contacted by guides. He began to see auras and received the first of many prophecies. Often, Scallion received many of his messages in dream state, and sometimes they even appeared on his computer screen from an entity named Matrix. Eventually, he told his remarkable story in *Notes From the Cosmos*. Currently, Scallion runs the Matrix Institute which publishes *The Earth Change Report*.

What does Gordon Michael Scallion see for the future? His predictions for the future chronicled in *Notes From the Cosmos* include severe earth changes in California and economic decline from 1998 to 2012, followed by a new spiritual awareness: "After difficult times at the end of the century and the beginning of the next, society begins to emerge as a spiritually conscious community. Wars are replaced by a spirit of cooperation. Food is shared globally through a system of food banks. Life in the new millennium is based on unity and respect for all life. If you were to ask various national leaders in the next millennium, "What do you consider your country's most valuable treasure?" Most would respond emphatically, "Our children!"[9]

The planet has been going through changes since the 1970s, but in the past decade things have been accelerating. The time has passed when the earth changes can be stopped. They have been held back, however. Originally, Scallion felt the major earth changes would be complete by 2001—but now he had given the date of 2012. He has even published a maps of the earth after the major changes which he continually updates on his website: www. matrixinstitute.com.

Some of these earth changes will be to due to a series of earthquakes, including a mega one in California, and global warming. The weather also becomes erratic with "dry places wet, and wet places dry." On the new map of the United States, Florida and much of the West Coast disappears—California becoming a series of islands. Seventy-five percent of the those who do survive, will be children according to Scallion's guides. Camps will be set up in five states to deal with the large number of homeless children. The economy and government of the United States collapses and the nation once again becomes a nation of colonies.[10]

Annie Kirkwood, a contemporary of Scallion's sees many of the same earth changes. Kirkwood began receiving messages from Mother Mary in 1987, after she read Jean K. Foster's *The Mind-God Connection*. Soon the middle-aged housewife was smelling roses and sensing the very real presence of Mother Mary. When the mother of Jesus approached her, Annie Kirkwood protested, "I am not Catholic." Mother Mary answered, "Nor am I."

Like Scallion, she predicts there will be a period of the three days of darkness and difficult times ahead. She also sees geographical and economic upheaval. In an interview in 1997, Annie Kirkwood explained that, "Many of the predicted disasters have been delayed five to ten years from this year. This is happening because people are truly making changes within their hearts. As more people change, a planetary shift in consciousness will occur. It is beginning to shift, but we haven't accomplished it completely.[10] Her husband, Brian Kirkwood, who believes that that earth changes will eventually occur, wrote a book, *A Survival Guide for the New Millennium*, which emphasized storing food, water, and medical supplies, along with alterative sources of energy such as a generator.

Finally, on the tongues of angels comes abiding wisdom. They warn that we take in too much negativity from television. Even the news can be a bad thing if it leaves a negative residue in your mind. We can choose to be positive or negative. For many, the shift of consciousness is overwhelming as they turn to drugs, promiscuity, or mental illness out of the fear of these changes.

One of the leading channelers of angels is Ronna Herman, who has been receiving messages from Archangel, Michael. In 1997, she published her first book, *On the Wings of Light*. A retired business executive and real estate broker, she began a second career as a spiritual teacher and counselor. Herman's spiritual search began in the early 70s, and overcoming many personal losses, she now devotes her time to channeling Archangel Michael—sometimes channeling six days a week, seven to nine hours a day.

Citing recent tragedies, Ronna Herman sees a new compassion coming in: "Examples of this are the bombing of the World Trade Center in New York, the riots in the once sacred, beautiful city of Angels, Los Angeles, and the devastating bombing in Oklahoma City, as well as the violence and havoc experienced in other areas around the world. The Light frequencies hit the dark and exploded in a dynamic fashion. Out of the chaos and suffering came a new sense of unity, a clearing and cleansing and an opening of the heart center of those directly involved, creating a rippling effect much as a stone thrown in a pond.[11] Archangel Michael reassures that if we only can remain loyal to the Light, it is sufficient: "If you do nothing more than anchor the refined Light from the Creator which is radiating forth in higher and higher frequency patterns, it will be enough."

Futurist: Gordon Michael Scallion. Courtesy of MatrixInstitute.com.

Chapter Ten:
Medical Mediums

"People who have a deep inner yearning to ... heal the sick ... take away pain and stress ... who possess compassion ... are generous in nature ... willing to render service without remuneration ... only need attunement with spirit force of healing and give it practice."

—Harry Edwards

There is no more noble use of trance mediumship than that of healing. I have witnessed spectacular cases of medical mediumship, running the gamut from laying on of hands healing to psychic surgery. My husband, Ron, has been cured twice—once with the psychic surgery of Reverend Alex Orbito and the other invisible "procedure" of John of God, Brazil's leading medical medium. The healings—twelve years apart—were both remarkable.

We were introduced to Reverend Alex Orbito by our friend, Camille, who had spent several days in the Philippines observing psychic surgery. She assured us that Alex was genuine. Just the year before, I had shown my parapsychology class a film of Reverend Alex Orbito performing psychic surgery. The students and I watched in fascination as Reverend Orbito deftly entered the body with his bare hand to remove tumors and then magically closed the wound. I turned to the class, and said, "I can just tell you two things: I don't know how he does it; and yes, it is real."

With those two thoughts firmly in place, Ron, Camilla, and I left for Pennsylvania early one Thursday morning in the spring of 1992, to see the master psychic surgeon. The trip was the answer to a prayer. My husband had been severely injured in an accident on the job and had been out of work for three years with severe back pain. He described the pain, "It felt like I had an ice pick stuck in my back between my shoulder blades and pain so bad in my neck that I couldn't turn my head." He lived with constant pain in his neck and between his shoulder blades. Our family of six was barely surviving on Ron's workman's compensation and the small sum I managed to bring in from a part-time position as a psychology instructor. Naturally, we consulted a neurosurgeon who told us the cervical area was too sensitive to operate on, as an operation could result is paralysis. The surgery he preformed the year before, on the rotator cuff, had not provided Ron any relief.

With little to lose, we jumped at the change to see Reverend Alex Orbito in Pennsylvania that spring. We left about 7:30 am on Thursday and arrived in Lancaster about noon. The healings were scheduled at 2:00 pm. We merrily stopped at a lovely country inn near Lancaster for a gourmet lunch and arrived in a light-hearted mood. That mood changed quickly. Reverend Orbito, a short, middle-aged Filipino, spied Camille in the audience and selected her for the demonstration of psychic surgery. Before our amazed eyes he placed his bare hands in our friend's abdomen and made a five-inch incision without anesthetic. Camille, a tall red head, barely wiggled a toe. (Mentally, I made a note never to eat lunch before a session, as my stomach was decidedly queasy.) I turned to Ron for comfort, but his blue eyes were too focused on the scene unfolding in front of him to be aware of my discomfort.

Reverend Orbito, continued the treatment by placing an inch roll of white gauze into Camille's abdomen. Then he miraculously sealed the incision by placing his hand over her bare white stomach—with a minimum of effort and blood! Without missing a beat, he explained, "No matter how pure you are, you can pick up negativity anywhere. Negative energy will attach to the gauze so it can be safely removed."

I just barely caught his words—my mind was elsewhere. *If he doesn't take it out, Camille could die from septic shock*, I thought. Reverend Orbito sympathetically glanced in my direction as he continued his talk. "Don't worry this is a safe procedure. In a few minutes I will remove the gauze and the negativity." Sure enough, he opened Camille's abdomen once again and removed the gauze which was now pitch black! I ask Camille how she felt afterwards, and she answered happily, "Buzzed out!"

With the demonstration over, about forty of us lined up for our treatment. I was excited, but nervous, as I put my head down on the table. Quickly Alex worked on my heart entering through the sternum. He seemed to hold the organ in his hands and literally was massaging it. His assistant, a tiny Filipino woman dressed spotlessly in white, held a kidney-shaped dish to collect the blood and tissue. While I felt some pressure, there was no real pain. Also, I was a little sensitive when he worked on my third eye—his finger digging in about an inch. By the end of the five minute session, I was grateful for the strong hands that helped me off the table. I, too, was "buzzed out." Afterwards, all three of us noticed pink "burn" marks in the areas which had been treated. A day or so later, these marks faded, leaving no permanent scars.

While I felt emotionally and spiritually recharged; Ron, on the other hand, who had suffered physical trauma to his neck and back received a miracle! After four psychic surgeries, his neck pain was completely gone and the pain between his should blade was lowered so it was much more tolerable! He was so well, he drove the four hours back to Connecticut without complaint!

What exactly is psychic surgery? D. R. Kartikeyan, former Director General of the National Human Rights Commission and an ex-cop gives this account: "Initially I wondered, how can this be? The body is entered with bare hands! So I wanted to experience it to ascertain that it's not an illusion, since I've been a lawyer and police officer all my life. I even had photographs and a video taken. Alex massaged my tummy and within no time I felt his fingers inside my stomach! I felt the blood. Then a pinching sensation. But no pain, no incision, no stitching."[1] Researchers Henry Belk, Stanley Krippner, and Andrija Puharich concur that psychic surgery is a genuine phenomena.

Psychic surgery is but one phase of medical mediumship which includes laying on of hands, medical clairvoyance, as well as psychic surgery. The first, laying on of hands healing does not require full trance, but can be done in an light altered state. England's Harry Edwards is the best example for this form of healing. Edwards (1893-1976) started his career as a printer. In his forties, he was introduced to healing when he visited a Spiritualist meeting. For over forty years he healed hopeless cases—often at a distance. Harry Edwards often sent out healing thoughts or prays for ill.

A typical account is that of a woman who came to Edwards's printing shop and told him that her husband was diagnosed with advanced lung cancer and was not expected to live. Ever sympathetic, Harry Edwards promised to send out absent healing thoughts. The woman returned to inform Edwards of a cure. Her husband, an agnostic by the way, knew nothing about Edward's prayers for him, yet the man fully recovered Convinced of the power of spiritual healing, Edward handed his business over to his brother-in-law and started the Sanctuary in Shere, South England in 1947. A sensible man, Edwards recommended cooperation between medical doctors and spiritual healers which still exists in England today.

As his fame grew, Edwards went on to cure thousands. His lectures at Royal Albert Hall in London were always packed—often as many as five thousand attended. Edward also wrote several books on Spiritualist healing, including, *The Power of Spiritual Healing* and *A Guide to the Understanding and Practice of Spiritual Healing*, as well as *Thirty Years as a Spiritual Healer* and the *Life of Jack Webber*.[2] Just as England's Harry Edwards exemplified the best of the "laying on of hands" healers, so America's Edgar Cayce is considered to be the best of the medical clairvoyants. Like Mr. Edwards, Cayce began his own group called the Association for Research and Enlightenment. Cayce was dubbed "the Sleeping Prophet" because twice a day, he would position himself on the couch in his office and enter a trance state for the purposes of medical clairvoyance.

Many of his patients, like Elsie Sechrist, were given little time to live by their physicians. Mrs. Sechrist was just a young bride when doctors diagnosed her with an incurable heart condition. She decided to have a reading with Edgar Cayce which not only provided a cure for her heart condition, but changed the direction of her life as well. Grateful for a second chance at life, Elsie Sechrist penned two books on Edgar Cayce's work: *Dreams: you Magic Mirror* and *Meditation: Gateway to Light*.

Edgar Cayce, "the Sleeping Prophet," was also an early advocate of the holistic approach to medicine. In one reading, his guides explained that the electromagnetic nature of man is made up atoms, which form organs that have their own electronic vibration. When cells can no longer reproduce, disease occurs: "When a force in any organ or element of the body becomes deficient in its ability to reproduce the equilibrium necessary for the substance of physical existence and its reproduction, that portion becomes deficient in electronic energy. This may come by injury or by disease, received by external forces. It may come from internal forces through lack of eliminations produced in the system to meet its requirements of the body."[3]

Edgar Cayce further explained that illness results from imbalances which may occur in this life or a previous life. For example, one woman who was crippled with a deformed hip was told that she had once watched the Christians being torn apart by lions as a spectacle sport. Another man was so depraved, he was confined to his room and had to rely on the care of Christian charity. Cayce said he was no less than the Emperor Nero returned, and his nurse who, by the way, had requested the reading, was told that she had been one of the early Christians. Cayce advised her to stay on the job, as much karma would be balanced for both the patient and the nurse.

Finally, there is the most rare form of medical mediumship—psychic surgery. There have been three well documented psychic surgeons: Jose Arigo, Alex Orbito, and John of God. John of God is very active in his native Brazil; while Reverend Alex Orbito continues to practice in the Philippines. Jose Arigo, however, died in 1972, at the age of forty nine in a car crash just as his work was becoming known in the West through John G. Fuller's book, *Arigo: Surgeon of the Rusty Knife*. In the book, Dr. Andrija Puharich testified: "It was the first time in my life when I've seen a scene like this. Where one minute from the time a patient steps up until the time he leaves, he either receives a prescription or an actual operation and walks out without any pain or disablement.[4]

Jose Arigo (1918-1971) first became aware of his gifts when he saw a dying relative being read the last rites: "As the last rites were being read, with no hope or knowledge of a cure, Jose' grabbed a knife from the kitchen and promptly removed a huge tumor from the women. The women recovered and a new life had begun for Jose."[5] Arigo's fame soon spread.

How did he do these psychic surgeries? Arigo claimed he was a channel for the spirit of a German doctor, Adolphus Fritz, who took over his body and performed the surgeries. Apparently, Dr. Fritz was an incredible surgeon who used few implements: As Judge Filippe Immesi reported after his visit to Jose' in prison, where he was permitted to continue to treat people: "I saw him pick up ... a pair of nail scissors. He wiped them on his shirt and used no disinfectant. I saw him then cut straight into the cornea of the patient's eye. She did not flinch, although perfectly conscious. The cataract was out in seconds ... Arigo said a prayer and a few drops of liquid appeared on the cotton in his hand. He wiped the women's eye with it and she was cured."[6] In the tragic accident that took his life in 1971, Jose Arigo, age forty-nine, left a rich legacy of medical successes complete with spirit diagnosis, herbals cures, and psychic surgery.

Just about this time, another psychic surgeon was becoming known for his work, Reverend Alex Orbito. He was introduced to the United States through Shirley MacLaine's book, *Going Within: A Guide for Inner Transformation*. According to Shirley MacLaine, Reverend Orbito's procedures are painless, and though the surgery is conducted without sterile conditions, patients do not develop infections.

Reverend Orbiton was born November 25, 1940, in the Philippines, the fourteenth child to a farmer and his wife. He began healing at fourteen when he cured a neighbor who had been paralyzed for ten years. With the magnetic intensity of a laser, using only bare hands, or in some cases a crude instrument, he opens the body to do the surgery needed. His powerful magnetism acts as an anesthetic and it also draws the blood away, so there is a minimum of bleeding. D. R. Karthikeyan—former Director General of the National Human Rights Commission—witnessed his bare-hands surgery at close quarters: "This was surgery with bare hands, without hypnosis, anesthesia, pain, or infection! Truly a phenomenon of mind over matter..."[7]

Perhaps the best known and most active psychic surgeon in the world today is John of God. João (John) was born in 1942, to a poor family in Brazil. As a child, Saint Theresa appeared to him in a vision and told him that he was healer and would always have this gift as long as he did not charge for his services. Later, at sixteen, the "entity" of King Solomon entered his body, and began performing healing as predicted by a vision he had received from Saint Teresa.

Since then, many other spirit guides have come through for healing—Dom Inacio de Loyola, a fifteenth century Spanish nobleman; Dr. Oswaldo Cruz, who helped to eradicate yellow fever; and the late Dr. Augusto de Almeida, a meticulous surgeon. About twenty-seven years ago, after years as a healer, he took residence in Abadiania and became known as "John of God." In 1991, John of God was honored by the President of Peru for healing over 20,000 of the nation's ill—including the President who suffered with atrophy of the hands, and his son who was diagnosed with a mental disorder. The President of Peru was so grateful that he awarded John of God the medal of honor.

John of God heals with two methods. First, the invisible surgery such as the procedure my husband received, and second, the visible surgeries which are graphic with incision, bleeding, and stitches. Recently, *Primetime* did a special where they witnessed a surgery in which João/John of God took four-inch gauze-tipped steel forceps, dipped them in a solution he calls "holy water," and shoved the forceps all the way up a patient's nostril and twisted them violently."[8] The patient reported the surgery to be painless with good results.

Most people seem to need to *see* visible surgery to confirm their healing, However, the invisible is just as reliable. When Ron and I visited John of God for three days in Atlanta in April of 2005, we both had invisible procedures. We left immediately afterwards to rest in our hotel room where we fell into a deep sleep. Every now and then, I would open my eyes to see the spirit forms of John of God's helpers from the other side watching over us. These spirits were just making sure the healing was complete. My husband was particularly impressed when he returned home to discover that a tumor about the size of a golf ball had completely disappeared without any visible surgery!

Harry Edwards. Courtesy of Harry Edward's Healing Sanctuary.

Author with Reverend Alex Orbito.

Chapter Eleven:
Trumpet Séances

"The highest good is like water. Water gives life to the ten thousand things and does not strive. It flows in places men reject and so is like the Tao."

—Tao Te Ching

Once mediums master trance, they can progress to other forms of mediumship, such as the trumpet séance. A trumpet is a cone-shaped instrument usually made of aluminum, although some mediums prefer copper. Basically, the trumpet acts as a megaphone through which a spirit can speak. In the heyday of Spiritualism, the trumpet would "float" about the darkened room (sometimes with luminous bands around it so it could be seen better), with "spirit" voices emanating through it. Of course, not all trumpet mediums were genuine, some employed telescopic rods to manipulate the trumpet in a totally dark room. Fake mediums would then pitch their voices to sound like "grandmother" or "Aunt Ann." However, just as true trance mediums exist, so do genuine trumpet mediums.

The trick is to find a real trumpet medium. When I asked Reverend Gail Hicks where to find a good trumpet teacher, she advised, "If you want to study trumpet séance, Camp Chesterfield is the place to go," and then added, "See my teacher Suzanne Greer—she's one of the best." Instantly the hair went up on my arms—a sure sign that spirit was guiding me.

However, before I embarked on a trip to Chesterfield, Indiana, I did some research. According to Camp Chesterfield's website, the camp was the result of Dr. John Westerfield's interest in mesmerism, phrenology, trance speaking, healing, clairvoyance, and spirit contact. In 1843, he sponsored lectures at his newly built Union Hall in Anderson, Indiana. In 1855, seven years after Spiritualism began, John and Mary Ellen Bussel Westerfield turned to mediums when their only child, John, Jr., passed to spirit at age fourteen. As interest in trance mediums, healers, psychic spirit artists, and trumpet and materialization mediums grew during the late 1880s, Dr. and Mrs. Westerfield were inspired to form the Indiana Spiritualist Association in 1883. Often the group met on the banks of the White River. In 1891, they purchased land there to form Camp Chesterfield so that Indiana's Spiritualists would have a place to meet. Many Spiritualist camps, including Lily Dale Assembly formed in 1879, came into being during this period as a private place to meet and practice mediumship.

In fact, mediumship was not legal until recent years. As late as the 1950s, a medium could be arrested for giving messages in public. No wonder the Indiana Spiritualists had a saying: "You're not a real Spiritualist until you have been arrested!" In fact, Mr. Hett, an Indiana police officer was about to arrest a Spiritualist medium, when she gave him an evidential message from his deceased son. Hett changed his views on mediumship and became an ardent Spiritualist, who later donated the funds to build the Hett Art Gallery and Museum in 1954.

The gallery features an extensive collection of portraits precipitated by mediums Elizabeth and Mary Bangs. Many of the portraits were precipitated in full day light in the late 1800s and early 1900s. Artifacts from the Fox sisters and other early Spiritualist psychic photos can be found there, including slates on which spirits wrote messages. Typically, a piece of chalk was placed inside a pair of school slates. Then the spirits would be invoked. Often, participants heard the scratching sounds of chalk. When the noises stopped and the two slates were untied, spirit messages would be revealed in the handwriting of deceased loved ones. This amazing aspect of physical mediumship was commonplace at the turn of the century.

Much the collection goes back to the late 1800s and early 1900s. However, during the 1920s, and again in the late 1960s, interest in mediumship and psychic phenomena peaked with large numbers attending events at Camp Chesterfield. Unfortunately, some unscrupulous mediums who faked materialization and trumpet mediumship entered the camp in the 1960s and early 1970s. When Lamar Keene wrote an expose, *Psychic Mafia*, interest in trumpet mediumship and materializations declined. According to Lamar Keene, mediums at Camp Chesterfield kept index cards on regular camp attendees in an office beneath the Cathedral. When asked about the huge office underneath the Cathedral, Reverend Suzanne Greer, a Camp Chesterfield veteran, just laughed and commented, "Sometimes I take groups of students down to the cathedral basement just to show them there are no file cabinets tucked away there!"

Sadly, the negative publicity has taken a toll on the camp. By the time Ron and I arrived at Camp Chesterfield in April 2005, only a handful of students were attending classes and the camp appeared much as it did fifty years ago. Row upon row of small cottages lined the streets with a main office building greeting visitors at the entrance of the camp. The cafeteria and Hett Art Gallery and Museum are to the left. The Western Hotel where visitors can get a room with twin beds for thirty-five dollars or dorm room for fifteen dollars a night are to the far left. Classes were equally affordable at ten dollars for a trance or trumpet class. We signed up for classes in meditation with Reverend Patricia Kennedy, and "Introduction to the Séance Room," with Reverend Suzanne Greer, as well as two trumpet séances.

Our first trumpet séance was with Reverend Louise Irvine, a charming spry eighty-year-old medium. To be sure, she got two huge trumpets up during her two-hour Ascended Masters Séance. I was impressed, to say the least, as each master came through with their beautiful philosophy. At the end, the Master apported about twenty or so stones. While, Ron felt the stones looked suspiciously like those sold at the local rock shop, I decided to hold judgment.

Our next trumpet séance with Reverend Suzanne Greer culminated a week long seminar: "Introduction to the Séance Room." Suzanne Greer knows her trade well; she sat in a development circle for fifteen years to become a trumpet medium. During the week, Reverend Greer patiently acquainted us with the necessary information needed to build a medium's cabinet and set up a séance room. We were again advised that "like attracts like." In order to attract a high guide, we needed to avoid alcohol, drugs, and negativity. "A negative person can affect the whole séance," solemnly warned Suzanne. People must be respectful and on time. To make her point, she stated, "You absolutely have the right to turn someone away. One summer evening, a later-comer rang Reverend Bill English's (the noted trumpet medium) door before a trumpet séance. The woman insisted, "My guide says I have to go to your trumpet séance." Reverend English firmly closed the door, with the wry comment: "Well, your guide didn't tell me!"

An orderly environment is essential for a séance. It is a team effort between sitter, medium, and spirit. Besides having sitters arrive on time, it is important to maintain an orderly séance in an uncluttered, clean, pleasant room. Guides often like incense and fresh flowers, as well as religious icons and musical instruments to be present. These are requests—not demands. The one point that Reverend Greer drilled into us was, "You control spirit, spirit does not control you!"

Finally, after a week of study, our class of twelve, which included several veteran mediums and advanced students, was allowed to visit the séance room. We excitedly gathered in Reverend Greer's basement where she had set up her séance room. Basically, it was a twelve by fourteen room with a cabinet that consisted of a two foot by three foot closet, closed in on three side with the front curtained off. The curtain is closed so that ectoplasm can build up in the small space when the medium is in trance.

Twelve chairs were placed in a circle with a mediums' cabinet at the back of the room. We took our places in the circle and Reverend Greer sat down in the cabinet, closing the curtain. Suzanne uses two large trumpets, each weighing several pounds. Both trumpets sat on a table in front of the cabinet. The lights were dimmed and five minutes of silence ensued.

Soon, the silence was broken by the child-like voice of Reverend Greer's joy guide, Penny, urging us to sing to bring up the vibration. We cheerfully sang our favorite camp songs in order to raise the vibration. Before long, two three-foot trumpets were up and making their way around the room. When a trumpet stopped at me, I received messages from Kenneth and Gladys Custance, among other spirits who gathered in her basement séance room. Their voices were audible and could be heard by all in the room.

At the end, Reverend Greer lowered the trumpets so they touched our toes, for those who had poor night vision. While Ron saw the two trumpets, clearly, I appreciated the tap on the toes.

How exactly does spirit manipulate the trumpet? Basically, the ectoplasm is extracted from the entranced medium and then ectoplasm forms etheric cords or spirit hands which wrap around the trumpet. Since ectoplasm is sensitive to light, most mediums prefer to work in total darkness. British medium, Jack Webber, was photographed with hand and legs tied to a chair with ectoplasm extruding from his neck and solar plexus and trumpets supported by cords of ectoplasm—one from his mouth and the other extending from his navel. This picture, published in Harry Edward's biography, *Jack Webber*, is unusual because ectoplasm, which is sensitive to light, can only be taken with infrared film.

According to Reverend Chester Bias—who was a Camp Chesterfield medium before he moved to Manhattan—trumpet mediumship requires a strong spirit guide and a medium with the ability to go into a "dead" trance. While in trance, the spirit workers create rods or hands from ectoplasm to lift the trumpet of Chester Bias's students. Reverend Hoyt Robiniette gave an exceptional demonstration of trumpet mediumship on July 27, 2006.

Reverend Gail Hicks, my husband, Ron, and I had the privilege of attending one of his phenomenal trumpet séances. Twelve of us gathered enthusiastically in the basement of the lovely suburban home in Franklin, Massachusetts. Reverend Robinette went quickly into trance as we repeated the words to the Lord's Prayer. Soon Dr. Kenner, his guide, was in control of Reverend Robinette's body. We all heard his voice come through the trumpet as clearly as if it had been broadcast on television. Dr. Nelson, Reverend Gail Hick's guide, came through with a distinct British accent, as did my guide, Harry Edwards. This was the third contact that I had had with Mr. Edwards.

The first meeting took place in June of 2006, during a private sitting with Reverend Hoyt Robinette. At that time, the spirit of Harry Edwards came in to encourage my work as a medical clairvoyant, adding that he would be available to guide me from the other side. The next evening, I attended a spirit card séance with Reverend Robinette. As if to prove his intentions, the face of Harry Edwards manifested on my spirit card. Naturally, I was thrilled to hear his voice from the trumpet: "My name is Harry Edwards. I knew of Dr. Kenner [Reverend Robinette's guide] many moons ago. We are like brothers."

He then gave this advice: "I have always believed in affirmations. You will have opportunities to get the gifts of healing and to pass it on to others." Not only could I hear the voice, but so could everyone else in the room. Next, he gave me the opportunity to ask a question. Since I had been thinking about this on the ride down, I knew exactly the one I would ask. Without hesitation, I asked the master healer himself: "I want to be a medical clairvoyant. What would you advise?" Harry Edwards answered, "You are going out of the body and then Mr. Edwards [referring to himself] will come and help." All the others had messages from their guides as well—except Ron, who had staunchly announced in the car that he had no question in mind. Apparently, we were not alone on the three-hour drive down. By the end of the evening, we all felt as if we had been floating on a cloud between this world and the next!

Margery Crandon during a séance.
Courtesy of PrairieGhosts.com.

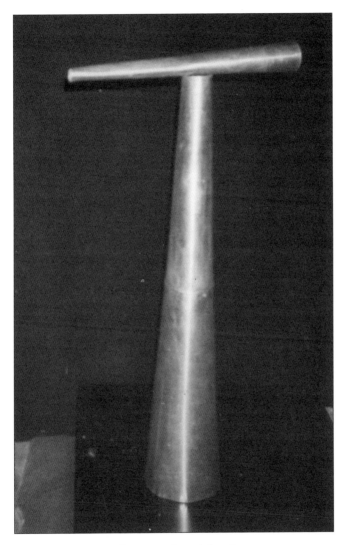

Aluminum cones or "trumpets" used for séances.

Chapter Twelve:
Spirit Art—Precipitated Paintings Spirit Cards, and Pictures on Silk

"There is no religion higher than truth."

—Madame Helena Blavatsky

Physical mediumship can be heard, seen, and photographed—even apported. However, nowhere have I found more tangible proof than in the spirit cards of Reverend Hoyt Robinette, along with the work of spirit artists Reverend Phyllis Kennedy Reverend, Rita Berkowitz, and the trance mediumship of Maria Getrudes. Spirit art is not new. At the turn of the century, it was in full bloom with the precipitated paintings of the Bangs sisters and the Campbell brothers in the United States.

Spirit art may be accomplished by many methods. A guide or loved one may be seen clairvoyantly by a medium with artistic ability who then sketches or paints the image. English artist, Coral Polge, who is known for her drawings of deceased loved ones, employs this technique. Another method is trance mediumship in which an artist from the other side takes over the body of a medium and does the work directly. Brazilian spirit artist Maria Getrudes is famous for this approach. A third method of spirit art involves no human hands whatsoever. Here spirit directly precipitates pictures, including portraits of deceased loved ones and guides, directly on cards.

The best known of the first type of spirit artists is Coral Polge of England. As psychic artist Coral Polge drew portraits of spirits who contacted her through the guidance of seventeenth century French painter Maurice de la Tour. According to Ms. Polge, "I don't actually see the person I am drawing, I am rather drawing what I feel than what I see. It's something about the personality I am drawing that comes over me and it is developing as I am drawing."[1] While drawing, she is quite sensitive to the vibrations of both the spirit and material world. Coral Polge explains, "Everything, my surroundings, my state of balance, even the weather can affect it. So sometimes my work can be quite brilliant, other days it just doesn't work and I start wondering if I lost the gift. As a medium you are always a channel and not always the most perfect channel. But there are days when you connect so clearly that you surprise yourself."[2]

Over several decades, in the 1960s, '70s, '80 and '90s, Coral Polge drew pictures of the deceased for those who flocked to her public demonstrations in England. Mrs. Bayles of Rhodesia could not attend these demonstrations; however, her request was honored. She received a portrait of her son who had died as a teenager during a routine operation. His spirit appeared to Coral Polge who captured his likeness, much to his mother's delight.

Polge joined the world of spirit on April 29, 2001. Her colleague, Stephan O'Brien, wrote lovingly of her after fifty-four years of mediumship in *Psychic News*: "She raised the spiritual awareness of her audience. Huge crowds of people sat entranced as from out of nowhere their loved ones' faces appeared again before their tearful eyes."[3] Her amazing story is told in her biography, *Living Images*, which was coauthored with Kay Hunter.

While I never had the privilege of meeting Coral Polge, I have had the pleasure of having a spirit portrait drawn by Reverend Phyllis Kennedy of Camp Chesterfield in 2005. It was just about this time that I had started teaching a course in Tibetan techniques of mediation and astral travel to students at the New England School of Metaphysics. Without realizing it, I had inadvertently attracted a new guide to my band—a young Tibetan tulku. When I visited Reverend Kennedy, I was delighted with this portrait of my Tibetan guide. This was not the first time I had had a spirit artist paint a guide. A few years before, Reverend Gail Hicks did a charcoal sketch of a tall Egyptian guide—one I have seen since childhood. I have enjoyed taking several classes in spirit art and have made some rudimentary progress. I was particularly thrilled to find a picture of Margery Crandon on my canvas when I was impressed from the spirit side during one of Reverend Hick's classes.

Another spirit artist who has taught at the New England School of Metaphysics is Reverend Rita Berkowitz. In February of 2005, I was completing *Connecticut Ghosts* which I dedicated to my grandparents, Harry and Katherine Brickett. Reverend Rita visited for the first time that month. We had never met, nor had I discussed the book or my grandparents with her. Yet, she brought through an amazing likeness of my grandfather, Harry Brickett, on page 89.

Not all spirit artists are impressed by deceased relatives. Some, like Reverend Sherry Lee Caukins of Lily Dale, communicate with angels. Reverend Caulkins came from a family of Spiritualists. Having had several readings with her, I can attest to her unusual ability to tap into angels. Sherry Lee starts with a prayer and begins her communication. In about twenty to thirty minutes a finished picture is ready for interpretation. Precise to the month, she once noted an empty spot—July 15th to the end of August. "Blank space usually means not much is happening then," Sherry Lee explained. Her words were true, for as a college professor, I had time off during the period she mentioned.

Not only do drawings come from impressions of spirit, but some are also produced by invisible hands. Both Camp Chesterfield in Indiana and Lily Dale Assembly in New York house collections of slates with their original spirit messages. Slate writing was a another popular form of physical mediumship at the turn of the century. A pair of child's school slates would be tied together with a piece chalk placed in between. Sometimes the chalk would just be left on the table beside the slates to provide just the suggestion of chalk.

For those who were concerned about trickery, slates would even be locked to prevent any tampering. Reverend Gladys Custance, my teacher, attended a slate séance at Camp Chesterfield in Indiana in the 1950s. She did not often talk about phenomena. However, on one occasion, she told this story to our class. According to Gladys, each person would have a pair of children's slates. The sitter was instructed to place a piece of chalk in the middle and tie the two slates together. Then the lights were turned off and the medium went into trance. "All we could hear was the sound of chalk writing," said Gladys. Her husband, Reverend Kenneth Custance, their friend, Meroe Morse, and her mother, Celeste Osgood, also attended the séance. When the sounds of writing ceased, the mediums requested that the lights be switched on. Each sitter open their slates to find a message written by spirit hands. Some even recognized the handwriting! "Celeste, whose husband had recently passed on, received a note from Professor Osgood *in his own handwriting,*" Reverend Gladys Custance added with emphasis.

In addition to physical phenomena, spirit artists from the other side have been known to impress mediums. In Brazil, some of the world's leading deceased artists, such as Pablo Picasso, Joseph Turner, Vincent Van Gogh, and Claude Monet have also come through to continue their art via the entranced mediums. For example, Brazilian medium Luis Gasparetto reports Picasso, Degas, Van Gogh, and Monet continue to paint though him. He has been observed by audiences working in a light trance state completing his paintings in a matter of minutes. Observers say his works of art exhibit styles reminiscent of deceased painters. What is even more amazing, Gasparetto does these paintings in a darkened room. Sometimes he even paints a great work of art upside down!

In July of 2006, Ron and I, along with Mary Ardent and Nancy Ross, two students from the New England School of Metaphysics, attended the Brazilian weekend at Lily Dale in New York. We watched spell-bound as Maria Getrudes did her remarkable spirit art. Within minutes, the medium went into trance, and artists Claude Monet, Joseph Turner, and Vincent Van Gogh came through. While the medium's eyes were closed, the spirits took over the brush and completed masterpiece after masterpiece in a matter of moments. A picture of woman by Monet took about nine minutes, the longest time, while the rest much less time. Here is an example on page 140 courtesy of the Lily Dale Museum.

Even though it is wonderful to see spirit artists take over the body of a medium who has little artistic ability, it is even more amazing to witness paintings done without human hands, called precipitated paintings. While it is a rare event, spirit has been known to do this through the remarkable mediumship of the Bangs sisters, the Campbell brothers, and Reverend Hoyt Robinette. This type of rare, but real, physical mediumship seemed to be a thing of the past. For many, the precipitated paintings of the Bangs sisters and Campbell brothers were a wondrous icon of the heyday of Spiritualism. By the 1990s, few mediums even knew their names, and no one in Spiritualist circle really believed much in physical phenomena—except for a few out of the way camps, such as Camp Silver Bell in Pennsylvania and Camp Chesterfield in Indiana.

Fortunately, the Bangs sisters, who demonstrated clairvoyance, physical manifestation, and direct voice mediumship, left a legacy of precipitated paintings. The sisters grew up in a average Chicago family—their father was a postman, and their mother was a home-maker. However, the girls were born mediums. By the time the girls were five or so, they were manifesting pieces of coal. Soon, they were demonstrating rapping and voices from beyond only heard when the two young sisters were present. Later, more demonstra-tions came, such as physical manifestations, automatic writing, independent slate writing, clairvoyance, and clairaudience.

Lizzie and May Bangs are best remembered for "precipitated" spirit portraits. The sisters, who often spent the summer at the Lily Dale Assembly in New York, were able to precipitate these excellent likenesses of deceased relatives in about twenty minutes to three hours without ever touching the canvas. They began first by sitting in a dark room with a blank canvas. The background, figures, and finally details of a portrait would manifest frequently, often resembling the face of a deceased relative. Later, they were able to do the paintings in full day light. Most observers, like Mrs. Gertrude Bresian Hunt, did not take their eyes from the canvas: "I did not remove my eyes from the canvas, and would stake every-thing I possess that no hand touched the canvas after I placed it in the bright light of the window, until the picture was finished."

Mysterious events occurred in regard to the portraits. One involved Dr. Daughtery, who requested and received a portrait of his deceased wife, Lizzie. He was not pleased as his twin daughters were not in the picture. He was about to return the portrait when the two girls mysteriously manifested! Other examples of a super-normal manifestation occurred when a nearly completed portrait of baby "Bernal Tobias" opened and shut his eyes. The painted eyes then remained opened according to startled observers.[4]

Even their slate séances were fascinating. In *Glimpses of the Next State*, Admiral W. Usborne Moore describes one of their slate séances. This one took place in 1908, in a slate séance with Miss May Bangs. Admiral Usborne Moore brought along his questions in a sealed envelope and placed the envelope, which also contained several numbered sheets of blank paper, between two slates tied together with rubber bands. For about a half hour the séance continued. Miss Bangs then opened the slates, and she returned his envelope still sealed. Admiral Moore was amazed when he slit opened the envelope. "I slit open the end of the envelope with my pen knife, and found, besides my questions, nine and half pages of the blank paper covered with ink, as if with a steel pen, duly numbered, and written at the instance of the spirit friends to whom I had addressed four of the five questions, and signed in full. The replies were categorical, giving or confirming information of great value to me personally; referring to facts and happening of forty years ago, which the spirit and I alone were aware of; and adding the names of individuals whom I had not named in my questions, but whom we both knew in the past and who had participated in the events referred to by me.[5]

At the close of the last century, another duo, the Campbell brothers, became well known in Spiritualists circles for their pre-cipitated paintings. The Campbell brothers were actually Allen Campbell, born in England in 1833 and died in Atlantic City in 1919, and Charles Shourds, an American whose date of birth is unknown. Records indicate that he died at Lily Dale Assembly in 1926. Both men were export traders and New Jersey businessmen. They frequently gave séances in Lily Dale where they maintained a home on One Cottage Row and in Boston. By 1899, the Campbell Brothers were so celebrated that they sailed for Europe for engage-ments in England, Scotland, Germany, and France.

On February 6, 1897, the Spiritualist publication, *Banner of Light,* gave this account of their work which included, "over sixty typewritten messages" that were actually given by the spirit typewriter "all of which were signed with full names of those who have passed over and were messages full of love and consolation which are dearly cherished by the favorable recipients."[6] The *Banner of light* also reported that "six magnificent paintings were received on slates as well as "an exquisite miniature of Edwin Booth."[7]

Two of their most famous precipitated paintings, a portrait of Abraham Lincoln and one of "Azur, the Helper," now hang in the lobby of the Maplewood Hotel at Lily Dale. Ron Nagy, author of *Precipitated Spirit Paintings*, described the method by which the Abraham Lincoln painting was precipitated as follows: "The method of reception was much the same as the Bangs sisters, except the canvas was placed on the table. The paints were placed in a receptacle beneath the table, then the table covered with black cloth to eliminate the light, leaving the frame and canvass alone exposed. The Campbell brothers sat with the sitters around the table, with hands on the table to produce a concentrated batter."[8] The result was a slowly precipitated painting which bore an amazing likeness to Abraham Lincoln. as you can see on page 139. The picture was precipitated in broad day light in full view of all the sitters.

Their largest and perhaps most beloved precipitated portrait was of Allen Campbell's spirit guide, an Old Testament master by the name of Azur, who had been with him since Campbell was a young medium. On June 15, 1889, the Campbell Brothers sat in their Egyptian séance room to begin the process of precipitation of a forty by sixty portrait of "Azur, the Helper," on pages 138 and 139.

After each person passed their hands over the blank canvas, Mr. Campbell took his seat in the séance cabinet where the canvas was placed. One by one, each of the sitters was allowed to spend some time in the cabinet with the medium. Several Spiritualists were present—Emma Prendergast, Abby Pettengill, Helen M. Sage, Sidney Kelsey, F. Comdon White, and Helen White. In a letter to the *Banner of Light* dated August 15, 1898, they testified, "Each time the curtain opened a partly finished picture of Azur could be seen. Slowly and methodically, the portrait of Azur the Helper formed."[9] Campbell then channeled wisdom and information on the stars to the group. More lights were brought in and the curtain lifted. There was Azur, life size with his arms uplifted as if giving a lecture.[10]

Trude Lamb, an inspirational artist from the 1940s, printed this information on her copy of a picture of Azur, "A bosom friend of Daniel in the *Bible*. Azur ended the discourse with this message: 'Be ye not seekers for signs but workers for the cause of the spirit of eternal truth.'"[11] Ron Nagy, curator of the Lily Dale Museum, has examined the portrait of Azur many times. He has found symbols embedded in Azur and other precipitated paintings, which remain fresh in color after a hundred years.

Today the closest medium to the Bangs sisters and Campbell brothers is Reverend Hoyt Robinette. I have attended several of his séances in Massachusetts, Connecticut, Maryland, and Indiana with good results. In the last two years, I have received six spirit cards—all evidence of his talents.

Reverend Robinette began his spirit card séances by opening a brand new package of three-by-five blank white index cards which were all examined by one of the sitters. He then held up a cobra basket about fifteen inches in width, made of woven tan reeds and lined with white cotton, to keep light out. Again, a member of the audience was called up to examine the basket carefully. Hoyt first placed a variety of colored pens and pencils with their caps secured in the basket; then he added some cards, and then more pens lasagna style. Finally, he carefully fit the lid over the cobra basket and left it on the table in back of him in full view of all the participants.

For the next hour the basket remained in view and untouched as Reverend Robinette did a traditional billet séance in which he psychically read twenty-five billets while blind-folded. When Hoyt announced, "Katherine is here," I did not raise my hand to show recognition of the name—after all Katherine is a common name. So Hoyt turned to the spirit of Katherine and said, "Who is that with you?" "Oh, Harry is here, too." My right hand shot up. "Those are my grandparents." A few minutes later, Hoyt announced, "Tiger is here." Ron called out, " That my father's nickname." By the time the cobra box was opened, we were pretty impressed!

At the conclusion of the billet séance, Hoyt turned and picked up the snake basket and began to hand the cards out. The one with "Ronald Kuzmeskus" had a lovely scene of an American Indian camp ground against a background of purple mountains. Several names were impressed on the back. For example, "Ashtar," which was the same name that had been given to Ron during the billet séance. My card had a picture of an dapper older gentleman who I sensed might have been one of my guides, whose names had been written on the back of my card—perhaps "Dr. Cathart." It is interesting to note that the picture was sketched in green and gray—the same colors I was wearing that evening! Several names were written on the back of the card, including many who had made an appearance during the billet séance. A guide, "Bright Star," had written her name on the card along with "Chief Kiokee, "Ezekial," "Dr. Elmer Cathart," and "Pocahantas" as you can see in the pictures on page 144. The students were equally impressed. Regina, a physician, received a precipitated picture of Mother Cabrini, a Catholic saint, whom she greatly admires, and Nancy, a nurse and alternative healer, received a picture of Edgar Cayce. Each picture was in color and vivid detail.

Reverend Robinette's gifts did not come easily. He sat in a development circle for thirteen years. As his work has progressed, he has gone from precipitating simple messages and drawing of flowers to cards with first and last names of loved ones and guides on one side and beautiful portrait of spirit guides on the other. Reverend Gail Hicks, who has experienced more than twenty spirit card séances, explained the process: "But as the years have progressed, our spirit doctors have suggested that Hoyt use three-by-five index cards and crayons, markers, colored pencils (with the tops on) so that they can dematerialize the ink and re-materialize it on the card. His cards have progressed from just one-sided drawing of flowers and a message written on the card with signatures from your loved ones—grandma, mom, dad and your spirit guides—to the one shown here, a full-colored portrait of a Spirit Guide, like my Protecter, Chief Sundancer with the peace pipe, and Dr. Nelson, my chemist. On the other side of the card is my name and my guides who signed it."

I was so pleased with the first séance I attended in October 2004, that I invited Reverend Robinette to conduct a séance at the New England School for Metaphysics in Suffield, Connecticut. I had emailed him, but had not heard back. Then one night I was watching *Psychic Detectives* on television, when I clairvoyantly saw a crew of spirit workers come into my living room, carefully measuring the room and furnishings. *What in the world is going on?* I thought. Then it dawned on me. "These are Hoyt's guides—guess he is going to do a séance here after all!" In a flash, I put through a call to Indiana. Hoyt, who had just returned from a trip, picked up the phone. "Yes, I am planning to come to Connecticut in May," he assured me.

That May of 2005, I had two more spirit card séances with Hoyt. In the first, I received an unusual card with a picture of my guide, the late Reverend Arthur Ford, a Monarch butterfly, Jesus, and a quarter Moon (Page 143). I was happy to have a confirmation of Arthur Ford's presence, but I wanted more. On the way down to the third séance, I sent the thought out: "Arthur Ford, if you are truly my guide, please sign my card." Sure enough, he did! (Page 144.)

By the fourth spirit card séance, which was held at Camp Chesterfield, Indiana, in July of 2005, I was no longer testing spirit. It is amazing what faith can do. I had just submitted my manuscript for *Connecticut Ghosts*. I had been able to obtain permission to use all the pictures I wished, save one that of Reverend Carl Hewitt, who had just passed away in February of the year. When I looked down at my spirit card that very warm July evening, I couldn't believe my eyes—there staring me in the face was a picture of Reverend Carl Hewitt with Reverend Chester Bias. Excited, I jumped up with the words; "That is Carl Hewitt!" Hoyt casually said, "Oh, you knew Carl, too." "Yes," I replied, "I was so sorry that I could not put his picture in my book—I just was not able to contact the photographer who had taken a picture of Carl." The next morning at the camp, Hoyt graciously handed me a manila envelope: "Here," he said, "you can use this picture of Carl Hewitt in your book."

Since then, other wonderful spirit cards have followed. The cards seem to evolve as I progress spiritually. For example, when we dedicated the school to a year's study of medical intuition, I received a spirit card with the picture of the late Harry Edwards, the famous British healer. Then, as I was doing the research on physical mediumship, I received a card that has a picture of the late Boston medium, Margery Crandon.

My husband, Ron, has received some wonderful spirit cards as well. His favorite is a portrait of his guide, Ashtar. When Ron first received notice that his guide's name was Ashtar, he asked me, "Who is Ashatar?" "That is Ashtar of The Ashtar Command," I answered with pride. Wouldn't you know it, his next spirit card was signed, *The Ashtar Commnand,* double underlined. Ashtar must have been listening in on our conversation!

Reverend Hoyt not only does spirit cards but photos on silk as well. Here, view two examples of his spirit photos on pages 141 and 145. My husband, Ron, was able to identify the dog on his silk photo, and he feels one of the figures may be that of an deceased aunt who believed in Spiritualism. As for me, I was thrilled to spy my Aunt Ruth who had passed over in 1953!

"Azur" picture precipitated by Campbell Brothers. Courtesy of Lily Dale Assembly.

Author sitting in front of picture of "Azur."

Abraham Lincoln, precipitated by the Campbell Brothers. Courtesy of Lily Dale Assembly.

Monet painting via Maria Getrudes. Courtesy of Lily Dale Assembly.

Ann Gamache (left) and Ceil Lewonchuh (right) holding slates with messages from Spirit.

Reverend Hoyt Robinette with cobra basket.

Spirit Card of Ashtar, Spirit Guide of Ron Kuzmeskus.

Back of Spirit Card with "The Ashtar Command" underlined.

Spirit Card with Arthur Ford, Spirit Guide of Elaine Kuzmeskus.

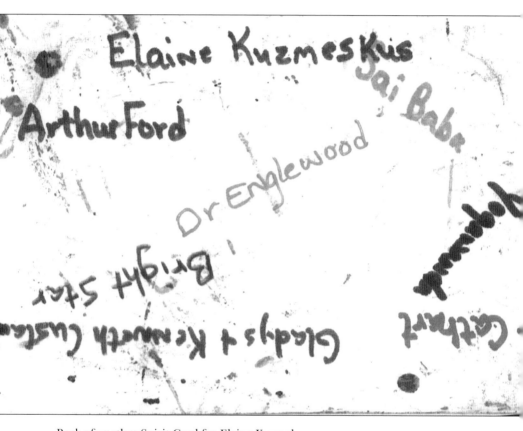

Back of another Spirit Card for Elaine Kuzmeksus.
Notice Arthur Ford's name with a red heart.

Photos on silk produced by Reverend Hoyt Robinett. Author was thrilled to see picture of her Aunt Ruth on the top.

Chapter Thirteen:
Materialization

"By far the most usual way of handling phenomena so novel that they would make for a serious rearrangement of our preconceptions is to ignore them altogether, or to abuse those who bear witness to them."

—Prof. William James

Spirit cards are a rare but real form of physical mediumship and so is materialization. I know, because not only did spirits speak directly to the twelve assembled at Reverend Hoyt Robinette's séance in July 2006, but they brought through materialized gifts known as apports. When the spirit of Harry Edwards, the British healer promised: "We have a gift for you—a gold cross with praying hands," my heart skipped a beat. Later, when the lights were turned back on, I spied a gold cross with praying hands laid next to the trumpet (Page 157). My husband, Ron, received a rock which had been carved to reveal a vein of amethyst, which his guide Ashtar had promised. Obviously, Ashtar knew of Ron's innate skepticism. His guide said, "At first glance, you will say it is just rock," and then added, "Like you, the rock is plain on the outside but very complex within." Other sitters received shells and gems of varying shades (Page 157). Our hostess, Reverend Gail Hicks, received a heart-shape gem which literally flew through the room and landed in a Kleenex box beside her chair!

The word "apport," comes from the French word which means "to bring." Spirit literally brings physical gifts such as feathers, jewelry, and coin through the trumpet. According to a spirit, White Hawk, "I speed up the atomic vibrations until (the objects) are disintegrated. Then they are brought here and I slow down the vibrations until they become solid again."[1]

Flowers can also be apported. Hilda Lewis was known as the "flower medium." Even when Lewis was a child, flowers would appear when she was present. Some believed that Saint Therese, known as "the Little Flower," brought them. She intrigued many in her day: "The last Professor D. Fraser-Harris was impressed by one experience. He saw a white cloud gather in the medium's lap. When the cloud cleared, there was a bunch of flowers in its place."[2] When asked what the experience was like, Hilda Lewis explained that she felt "labor pain" before the flowers materialized. According to Nandor Fodor, "The flowers were seasonal, very tightly packed, sealed with wax on the end, and always thornless."[3]

Many other mediums have been known to materialize flowers. However, one medium, Ethel Post Parrish of Camp Silver Belle in Pennsylvania, apported not only flowers, but a vase as well: "When the lights came on, we discovered that a large vase filled with gladiolus which had sat on the table in the middle of the room, had entirely disappeared. It was later found in the lobby of the Lodge. We asked Silver Belle about it on the following class night. The vase was of heavy pottery, and to remove that and the gladiolus seemed almost miraculous. This is Silver Belle's explanation—'I told you that it was hard work and it was. You see the vase and the flowers were of different vibrations. I had to dematerialize the flowers first and then when I got them out in the lobby, I materialized them again. I then came back and on a different rate of vibration did the same with the vase—then I put them together and set them on the table.' This seemed quite simple to her, but to us it was still incomprehensible—we knew that this wonderful phenomenon had happened, but we still could not understand how it was possible."[4]

Apports offer the most compelling evidence of spirit's presence. Some are common every day objects such are rocks or trinkets, but they often have deep significant meaning. Rev Keneth Custance who had a collection of over thirty apports told this story: a middle-aged lady, named "Marion," was gardening in California and lost the stone in her ring. Many years passed and she attended a séance which included apports at a Spiritualist camp. Lo and behold, the apport she received was the very stone she had lost many years ago!

A student, "Kathy," came to class with an even more intriguing story. Her uncle had been in Italy during the World War and had brought seven crosses home which he had had blessed by the Pope. One of the seven crosses was given to her grandmother who treasured it so much that she asked that it be placed in her coffin when she passed over. Later, Dr. Haber came to the Springfield Spiritualist Church and gave an apport séance. Sure enough, Kathy's apport was that very cross!

More recently, another student, Driana Buonanducci, told the class this apport story. A psychic herself, she began to wonder if she should continue this path of helping and healing others. That night, Sunday, August 13, 2006, as Drianna said her prayers, she asked Jesus for a sign. Three days later, August 16, 2006, her son Brandon told his mother, "You know that Buddha you love, Poppie broke it and glued it back together. Now there are angels wings sticking out of it." Drianna looked at the figurine of Buddha's head. Sure enough, there were wings sticking out of it!

She decided to crack the statute open to investigate further, and found not one, but four small figures of angles actually imbedded in the statute! (Page 170.) Remembering her heart-felt prayer, Drianna believes these apports were a sign to continue her psychic work.

Another favorite apport story comes from Reverend Gail Hicks of Fall River, Massachusetts. She and her sister, Reverend Charlene Hicks, and their friend, Bryan Lurie, decided to have a private séance. To prepare for the séance, Gail Hicks, explained, "I put out my quartz crystals, a big bowl of water and a basket of spirit cards." Then the trio sang and said The Lord's Prayer to raise the vibrations. On the floor before them was a basket, an unopened package of index cards, and some magic markers with the caps still on. Before the prayer was finished, they all heard a loud thud as something heavy dropped from thin air, onto the floor in the center of us. When they finished their song, Gail opened her eyes and saw "apports for each of us were placed on top; in the center of each of the quartz crystal clusters by our feet." Gail was overjoyed with her two-inch apport. On one side is a profile of an Native American, on the other a little sparrow (Her joy guide is named

Little Sparrow) and a picture of a Springer Spaniel—not unlike Gail's pet who had passed over.

The story does not end here. According to Gail, "The package of three-by-five cards—the kind you get in the store—still in the cellophane wrapper, was still there. When we opened the cards, we were high as a kite. There were seven or eight for each of us."

How did each one recognize their cards? "They had our names or the names of our guides on them. "The cards also had beautiful pictures on them. Gail described three cards vividly, "One had a map of the world after the earth changes; another, an architects drawing of how to make a portal to the other side, and Bryan's had a dragon on his!" Sometimes objects that are apported also have deep spiritual significance.

Sai Baba, whom many in India consider an avatar, once manifested a crucifix made from the original cross of Jesus for Dr. John Hissop, resident of the Satya Sai Baba Society in America. Sai Baba has been known to manifest rings, watches, and sacred ash, called vibuthi, for his many followers. He even manifested a miniature copy of the Behaved Gita for a Indian scientist.

Other masters of wisdom make their presence known through apported letters. Such was the case for Madame Blavatsky. The letters, were created many years before computers were invented, have computer-like marks. Madame Helen Blavatsky created quite a stir with the Theosophical Society when she presented the apported letters. On one occasion, the master Koot Hoomi wrote this note of encouragement to Mhini M. Chatterjee in Letter Eleven: "Never doubt, nor suspect, nor injure our agents by foul thoughts. Our modes of action are strange and unusual, and but too often liable to create suspicions. The latter is a snare and a temptation. Happy is he whose spiritual perceptions, ever whisper truth to him!"[5]

Not only have inanimate objects, such as letters and jewelry, been brought through the ethers, but live animals have also been apported. Emma Hardinge, in her book, *Modern American Spiritualism,* described the materialization of a white dove. Another medium, Margery Crandon, was credited with producing a live bird in her Boston séance room. When apporting animate matter, spirit has to use special methods, according to the laws of apports: "The Spirit Operators know how to change the vibration of matter so that it may be passed through other matter. In other words, they dematerialize the article they wish to apport and in its new state, they are able to pass it through solid matter—they then materialize it again after they have accomplished their purpose. They say that sometimes it is necessary to dematerialize a part of the wall or door so that the apport can pass through it in its original state. This method is used in the apporting of animate matter. Jesus understood this law and used it in many of his so-called miracles.[6]

Not only can spirit bring through apports, but sometimes the spirits themselves materialize. Naturally, being a medium, seeing spirit is a part of my every day life. However, occasionally I am caught off guard. While Ron and I were staying at the Arthur Findlay College in Stansted, we shared a small bedroom in the old section of the building. On the first night, I awoke to seeing a battalion of men dressed in medieval armor rushing through the room followed by a procession of nuns in ancient habits. Startled, I woke Ron up, "Do you see them?" I asked. "Yes," he answered, "now go back to sleep." Sometimes when visiting haunted places, you can literally tune into the former energy of the location.

There are times, though, when spirit will deliberately materialize during a séance. These materialization séances are rare; there were many more mediums who possessed the gift of materialization at the turn of the century. Materialization is not a new phenomena. The *Bible* mentions transfiguration on the Mount, when the spirits of Moses and Elias were seen.[8] (Mark, Chapter Nine) Jesus himself later materialized to his disciples. He encouraged them with the words, "Lo, I am with you always, even unto the end of the world." (Matthew 28:20)

One of the most documented cases of materialization mediumship was that of Florence Cook. Her phenomenal feat was verified by the eminent scientist Dr. Robert Crookes. While in trance, Cook materialized a little girl by the name of Katie King. By her own account from her spirit lips, she was "Annie Owens Morgan," the daughter of Sir Henry Morgan, a famous buccaneer. According Katie, she had married and had two children before she died at twenty-two or so. She also had turned to a life of crime—even murder—before she passed into spirit. While in spirit form, Katie even sat on Dr. Crookes's knee, and on another occasion, allowed a researcher to cut a bit of her etheric dress. She showed the researcher how dresses were mended in the spirit world: "One evening, when she was cutting off pieces of her dress rather lavishly, I remarked that it would require a great deal of mending. She answered, "I'll show you how we mend dresses in the Spirit World." She then doubled up the front breadth of her garment a dozen times, and cut two or three round holes in it. I am sure when she let it fall again there must have been thirty of forty holes, and Katie said, "Isn't that a nice cullender?" She then commenced, whilst we stood close to her, to shake her skirt gently about, and in a minute it was as perfect as before, without a hole to be seen.[7]

Another well-documented case of materialization at the turn of the century was that of the famous French medium, Marthe Beraud, who was known simply as Eva M. The daughter of a military officer, her unusual powers were discovered by General Noel, who later invited Professor Richet to investigate the medium. When in trance, spirits would materialize. A most frequent visitor was the spirit of her Hindu guide, Bien Boa, who was said to have lived three hundred years ago. The spirit materialized several times, allowing for an opportunity for a photograph. On one occasion, the spirit of a beautiful Egyptian girl materialized sufficiently for Professor Richet to cut a piece of her hair. Professor Richet in his *Thirty Years of Psychical Research*, explained "As I was about to cut a lock high up, a firm hand behind the curtain lowered mine so that I cut only about six inches from the end. As I was rather slow about doing this, she said in a low voice, 'quick, quick' and disappeared."[8]

In the United States, the Eddy Brothers of Vermont were known for their amazing materializations. Both Colonel Olcutt and Madame Blavatsky were impressed by what they witnessed at the Eddy brothers séances: "The procession of apparitions began drifting in and out of the Eddy cabinet on the schedule of every one to five minutes. The appearances of Honto and the Indians were slightly dim compared to Madame Blavatsky's peopled apparitions. "Hassan Aga," the wealthy merchant wearing a black Astarkhan cap and tasseled hood who said three times he had a secret to revel, but never did; "Safer Ali Bak," the man that guarded Helena for Nicephore Blavatsky in Erivan, now appearing as a Kurd warrior carrying a feathered spear; a Circassian *noukar* who bowed, smiled and said, "*Tchock yachtchi* (all right); a giant muscular black man in white-and-gold-horned headdress, a conjurer who she had met in Africa. "Madame Blavatsky's relative came through as well—her nurse and her beloved fat "Djadja."[9]

In more recent years, two extraordinary materialization mediums emerged—Helen Duncan in England and Ethel Post Parrish in United States. Both gave sitters who attended their séances the opportunity to see and talk to the materialized forms of their spirit loved ones. Thousands flocked to her séances in 1930s and 40s as both physical mediums were genuinely gifted.

However, Helen Duncan's life ended on a tragic note. The daughter of a cabinet maker, Duncan was born in Collander, a small Scottish town on November 25th, 1897. Her marriage to Henry Duncan was not an easy one. The couple had six children. Sadly, her husband became disabled during World War I, and Mrs. Duncan had to work at the local bleach factor by day and do her mediumship at night. She possessed the unusual gift of being able to effect materialization while in trance state. By the 1930s and 1940s, she was giving materialization séances throughout Britain. Her séances were a singular comfort to those who had lost loved ones in the war.

Unfortunately, Helen Duncan's gift was also her downfall. In the 1930s and 40s, Helen gave a séance at the Master Temple in Portsmouth, England. As mentioned prior, in 1931, she was fined for fraudulent mediumship—even though her control, Albert Stewart had tried to warn her. She continued her mediumship under the handicap of police surveillance.

Later in World War II, a young sailor with H. M. S. Barnum on his cap materialized. He said to his surprised mother, "Mum, the ship was sank and we were all killed." When Winston Churchill heard this, he was incensed at this breach of security and ordered the officials to find a means to prosecute her. The military found an archaic 1737 Witchcraft Act and prosecuted Helen Duncan, who was sentenced to six months in jail. Sadly, this remarkable physical medium was under police investigation until her death on December 6, 1956.

The United States has also been home to many talented mediums who possessed the gift of materialization at Camp Chesterfield in Indiana and Camp Silver Belle in Pennsylvania. Perhaps the most famous of the group was the late Ethel Post Parrish. She opened a camp in Ephrata, Pennsylvania in 1932—Camp Silver Belle—named for her Indian guide, Silver Belle. Lena Barnes Jefts gave this description of a materialization séance held August 8, 1943: "Silver Belle brought out three Spirit forms—the mother, father, and grandfather of Mrs. Emily Fritch of Reading, Pennsylvania. These three materialized Spirits walked from the cabinet to the front of the room, passing Mrs. Fritch, who remained by her chair near the other end of the room. Then they returned to her and the four conversed together for a few minutes. The three spirits returned to the cabinet; the two men preceding Mrs. Fritch's mother, who turned just before entering the cabinet to say a final Goodbye."[10]

While the spiritually minded accept these events as miracle, the more scientific may ask, "How can this be?" Silver Belle gave this explanation to Lena Barnes Jefts: "When we parted the curtains, we could plainly see Ethel Post-Parrish sitting in her chair apparently entranced. Silver Belle stood beside her, fully materialized, and in front of Silver Belle there was a mound of white, about two and one-half feet high—it looked like a snow bank but she told us that it was ectoplasm. She (Silver Belles) then proceeded to dip her hands into the mass and showed us how she was able to manipulate it in order to form the body and clothing of the manifesting Spirit."[11]

Materialization is not without its danger. It is vital for the health of the medium that no one interferes with this sensitive process. There is a story told at Camp Chesterfield regarding a medium who materialized the form of an attractive hula dancer who was dressed in only a Hawaiian skirt. One male sitter jumped up and touched the bare breast of the materialized form, not realizing the danger to the medium. Sadly, the medium died from an open wound to the abdomen—the spot where the ectoplasmic cord when been attached to the entranced medium.

Just how connected medium is to the materialized spirit was discovered in a carefully controlled experiment which was performed on Silver Belle by Doctor X. The doctor asked for permission to weigh the materialized Native American spirit. Silver Belle replied, "I tried to do what you asked but I am not sure your sister (Ethel Post-Parrish) can hold the body together for very long, so you had better hurry up." The doctor did hurry up, and when Silver Belle stepped on the scale, he saw the needle register thirty-five pounds. Another doctor, Doctor Z, proceeded to weigh the entranced medium and found that Ethel Post-Parrish weighed thirty-seven pounds less than when she first entered the séance room. Apparently, the thirty-seven pound loss would account for the materialization of Silver Belle with two pounds for the weight of the ectoplasmic cord which connected the materialized form to the body of the medium.[13]

On a humorous note, Silver Belle played a little trick on one of the regular sitters, Florence Harding. "Aunt Florence" always wore a red dress to the séance room to provide some color, as she knew that the spirit controls needed colored articles from which to draw the colors of their spirit garments. According to Lena Barnes Jefts, "One evening, a spirit came out showing large red roses on the ectoplasmic robes she was wearing. She was moving about the room, showing her robe to all the sitters, and as she returned to the cabinet, she said to Florence Hardy, "I drew the colors from your dress. Thank you." When Florence Hardy looked down there was a large white spot "as big as a saucer" in front of her dress. Silver Belle laughed at the trick and assured the dismayed sitter, "It will be all right when you go outside, Aunt Florence."[14]

Sadly, Camp Silver Belle is now closed.

In England, the Scole Group, who became rather noted for their psychic photographs, also experienced various materialization phenomena. In 1995, they saw spirit beings so solid, the fabric of their clothes could be felt as the spirits moved among the circle. One spirit voice was even heard to say, "Thank you for my chair."[15] One of the members of the group, Robin Foy, tells of a materialization séance he had attended with medium Stewart Alexander on August 30, 1992. Foy remembered the event: "During the course of the séance, my father, who had passed into spirit in 1987, materialized quite solidly. I was able to embrace him and recognize his face beyond a shadow of a doubt."[16]

While some will accept spirit raps, direct voice, and psychic photography as demonstrations of the survival, they balk at the very idea of materialization. Not so for Dr. Elisabeth Kubler-Ross. In 1970, a female spirit appeared before Dr. Kubler-Ross's eyes, and asked her, "Do you mind if we walk to your office?" Doctor Kubler-Ross followed the spirit to her office in the hospital: "But it was the strangest, most exciting walk I had ever taken. Was I having a psychotic episode? I had been under some stress, but certainly not enough to be seeing ghosts. Especially ghosts who stopped outside my office, opened the door, and let me enter first as if I was the visitor."[17] Upon closer examination, Dr. Kubler-Ross recognized the face of the spirit as Mrs. Schwartz, a patient who had died ten months earlier.

The spirit of Mrs. Swartz did indeed have a message for Dr. Kubler-Ross: "Dr. Ross, I had to come back for two reasons. Number one, to thank you and Reverend Gaines for all you have done for me. However, the second reason I have come back is to tell you not to give up your work on death and dying... not yet."[18] "Dr. Ross" decided to get some proof that this materialization was real, so she asked the spirit to write a letter to Reverend Gaines. Later, Dr. Kubler-Ross obtained hospital records to see if the signatures matched. When they did, Dr. Kubler-Ross made death and dying a life-long study.

While I have never personally witnessed a full materialization, I believe materialization is a possibility. Why? Because of this story told by my teacher, Reverend Gladys Custance, who did witness a full materialization at Camp Chesterfield in Indiana. According to Reverend Custance, "I saw the figure of my grandmother appear in the center of the séance room. She came over and talked to me. The spirit sounded like grandmother." Her grandmother's spirit asked for a harp to play. Gladys, a professional harpist, had an Irish harp with her, so she fetched it from the car. Her grandmother, accustomed to a larger concert harp, quipped: "My, it's shrunk!" Then grandmother's spirit asked, "Gladys, what would you like me to play?" Gladys answered with a twinkle in her eye, "Our favorite song." The spirit of her grandmother proceeded to play, Brahms Lullaby—the song they played every night before bedtime!

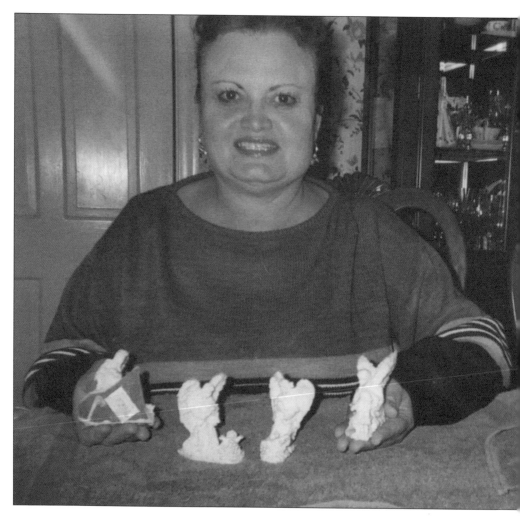

Apports received by Driana Buonanducci, West Hartford, Connecticut.

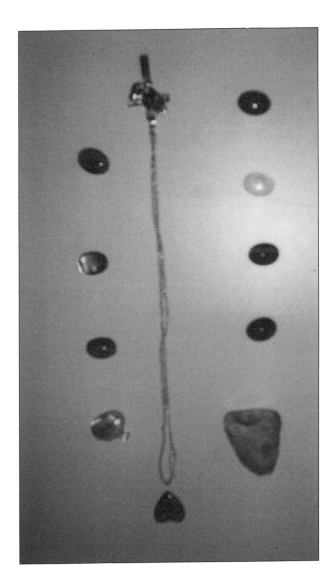

Group of apports materialized during July 27, 2006, at séance with Reverend Hoyt Robinette.

Apport received by Reverend Gail Hicks, Fall River, Massachusetts.

Chapter Fourteen:
Believe!

"Your belief will help create the fact."

—William James

Inevitably, when people witness great physical mediumship, be it spirit photography, psychic surgery, trumpet séances, or spirit cards, the first words out of their mouths are, "Is it magic?" How do observers distinguish between illusion and true spirit communication? How, for that matter, is the medium even sure that psychic phenomena is genuine?

A medium's first line of defense is his or her spiritual guide who protects the medium. Guides act as go-betweens when information is needed. For example, several years ago, the Goodspeed Opera House approached me to be the medium to conduct the 1997 Houdini séance. I had mixed feelings. First, I did not believe in public séances, since I felt that they were too sensational. As I tell my clients, I can't guarantee if loved ones will be present, but if they are in the room, I will bring them through. I was also concerned because it had been seventy-one years since Houdini's death, and he may well have incarnated during this period. I was about to decline the invitation when I heard a male voice advise, "Houdini has a message for you." Only then did I agree to do the 1997 Official Houdini Séance. The voice, by the way, was that of deceased medium Reverend Arthur Ford.

Next, a professional medium is able to gain rapport with spirit. The medium, after all, stands between the two worlds—the here and the hereafter. There are many ways of linking with the spirit world: psychometry, meditation, and trance, just to name a few. Sometimes it is as simple as tuning in though a picture or reading a biography of a deceased person. Such was the case for the Houdini Séance at the Goodspeede Opera House in 1997. I read *Houdini: His Legend and His Magic* by Doug Henning to tune into the great magician. As I turned the pages, I learned that Houdini would spend hours at the graves of other famous magicians. "He was trying to gain rapport with their spirits, too," I chuckled.

I also meditated on the many pictures of Harry Houdini which were in the book to increase rapport with his spirit. On Tuesday, October 28th, two nights before the séance was scheduled that first hour of October 31st,, I felt anxious. Why hadn't Houdini contacted me personally? I sent the thought out to my guides, "I need to see Houdini. It isn't fair to expect me to do the séance, and he has not come thought in person yet." They heard me. A few minutes later, the great magician appeared in the doorway of my bedroom, dressed in an elegant 1920s tuxedo. It seems he was ready for the show!

Finally, there is the evidence. When spirits come through, they give some evidence of survival—physical description, name, personality traits, or a message. Such was the case at the 1997 Official Houdini séance. We started by having everyone hold hands and focus on Harry Houdini. Once rapport with the spirit world was established, I began going around the table and giving messages to the twelve participants.

When I reached Timothy Gulan, the spirit of Harry Houdini came through to encourage the young actor in his craft. Houdini also mentioned to Timothy that he had been around the actor when he injured his shoulder and had decided not to go on. Houdini said he had been assisting him with the magic trick from spirit and urged him to go on anyway. Timothy did. In addition, Timothy Gulan acknowledged this message was true. Houdini had comments about the play, which he felt was too long and the humor needed a lot of work. With changes, he believed that the play could go onto Broadway.

If a message from Houdini was sufficient, the séance would have ended on a positive note. However, Sidney Radner, the director of the event, wanted more proof. He thrust an envelop in front of me, a move which I was not prepared for and demanded to know its contents. When I took the envelope in my hands, I used psychometry to sense the contents. Slowly, I answered, "A letter with Houdini's signature." When he acknowledged this and asked what the letter said, I went blank. Seeking more time to tap into psychic energy, I added, "I see an oak frame involved with the letter." "No, that's not correct," bellowed Radnor. (After the show, he admitted he did not know where the letter had been housed, and it could well have been under glass with an oak frame.) By this time, the spirit had had enough and the energy became quite thin. The many spirits who had been assisting me literally seemed to back away. Sidney Radner then took center stage and hammered home the point that the only official test of the Houdini séance to prove the existence Harry Houdini was to have the spirit of great magician open the handcuffs placed in front of the medium—a fact, like the surprise envelope that Radnar had conveniently neglected to mention to me. Since the handcuffs had not been opened by the spirit of Harry Houdini, Radnar deemed the séance a failure.

Do I think Houdini came through? Yes, just briefly for Timothy Gulan. After all, Houdini, who was childless, was quite fond of young people. Houdini did have a message which I brought through, along with about twenty other messages for the audience during the 11 pm message service. These messages, by the way, contained names and physical descriptions of deceased relatives—information which members of the audience confirmed. From a Spiritualist point of view, the purpose of the séance was to bring through his messages to prove the continuity of life, and that was accomplished. While the Houdini séance ended on a sour note, the research I put into it proved valuable. Until the Houdini séance I was only vaguely aware of the name, Margery Crandon. I knew she was a Boston medium, but not much else. In my research, I happened on a book by Doug Henning, *Houdini: His Legend and His Magic*, and I read it with fascination. The book told the tale of Houdini's meetings with Boston medium Margery Crandon. Intuitively I suspected Houdini's criticism of her talents was incorrect and unjust. Who would know if his comments were true or not?

Only one person came to mind—my minister, Reverend Kenneth Custance. He had been living in Boston during the 1920s, the heyday of Margery's mediumship. I decided to ask Kenneth the next time I saw him. Sure enough, I had the opportunity when I served at the First Spiritualist Church of Onset, Massachusetts, where Kenneth was still the pastor. One sunny fall day, as we were walking, I casually broached the subject: "Kenneth, you lived in Boston during the 1920s. Do you know anything about Margery Crandon?" A slow smile crossed his ninety-four year old face. "Yes," he answered. I continued, "Was Margery Crandon a genuine medium or was she a fake?" Since Kenneth and I had both seen our share of imposters, the question was not that unusual. Without hesitation, Reverend Custance replied: "She was the real thing!"

Margery Crandon was indeed "the real thing." No wonder *Scientific American* magazine and the American Society for Psychical Research considered her to be the best physical medium of 1923. Her direct voice and trumpet séances were so extraordinary that the English author, Arthur Findlay, termed her "the eighth wonder of the world." Unfortunately, in America she became a cruel joke when Harry Houdini mocked her mediumship on stage.

What happened between Harry Houdini, the great magician, and Margery Crandon, the last of the great physical mediums? Their two worlds collided, leaving years of hurt feelings and ill will in its aftermath. This is not surprising, since Harry Houdini and Margery Crandon came from completely diverse backgrounds. Houdini never finished high school and was largely self-educated. Margery, on the other hand, was married to a physician who taught at Harvard Medical School. Houdini was Jewish; while Margery, a gentile. He was a maverick and she belonged to Boston society. Even their drinking habits were opposite—Houdini was a teetotaler; Margery loved to party.

Their major difference, though, was their careers. Harry Houdini had carefully crafted his magic act, while Margery Crandon entered mediumship as a lark. His career was at its height; hers was just beginning. Their two worlds collided with catastrophic results for Margery Crandon. The *Scientific American* investigation committee was divided, and most members unsure of Margery's mediumship. The Boston Society for Psychical Research was so evenly divided that it eventually disbanded.

No wonder both she and Houdini were on very different paths. Harry Houdini was born Ehrich Weiss, the son Rabbi Mayer Samuel Weiss and his wife Cecelia on March 24 in Budapest, Hungary. The family emigrated to Appleton, Wisconsin, in the hope of a better life. Unfortunately, Rabbi Weiss did not fare well in Wisconsin and moved his family to a boarding house in New York City. Young Ehrich had to go to work at a variety of menial jobs to help support the family. While working at a necktie factory, he began practicing his magic tricks in earnest. Soon he teamed up with his brother, Theodore, to tour the vaudeville circuit with his act, "Metamorphosis." By 1900, Houdini was known as the "King of Handcuffs." He made several successful tours of Europe with his wife, Bess, as his assistant. Later, he stayed in the spotlight with his clever escape acts which included his famous Chinese Water Torture Trick.

Life seemed to be going well for the famous magician until his beloved mother, Celia, died in 1913. Later, Lady Jean Conan-Doyle would attempt to contact his mother with devastating results. His mother came through in English—a language she did not speak, and addressed him as " Harry" not the familiar "Ehrich."

While a Spiritualist would accept that Houdini's mother was mentally impressing Lady Doyle, Houdini, more of concrete thinker, simply dismissed the messages from his mother as false. While he tried to remain on cordial terms with Arthur Conan-Doyle, their divergent views on mediumship drove a wedge in their relationship.

Sir Arthur Conan-Doyle went on to champion Spiritualism; while Harry Houdini gained fame by debunking fake mediums. Houdini took pride in attending séances in disguise, and surprising the mediums, who worked in the dark, like Cecil Cook, with a flashlight. Cook, a New York trumpet medium, was discovered with a trumpet in his mouth when Houdini flashed a light! Often, Houdini hired others, such as Rose Mackenburg, to expose mediums. Rose went to mediums seeking to contact non-existent dead relatives, which the medium readily brought through for a fee. While some mediums were indeed fraudulent, others were probably poorly trained and unreliable.

Harry Houdini's only interest in being on the committee formed by *Scientific American* to investigate Margery Crandon was to disprove the evidence. In December 1922, the magazine had offered a five thousand dollar prize to anyone who could provide viable evidence of psychic phenomena. Margery Crandon was willing to do so and said she would not accept payment. Who was Margery the medium? She was actually Mina Crandon (1888-1941), who grew up on a farm in Ontario. After she moved to Boston, Mina met and married a grocer. The couple had one child, John. When the marriage ended in divorce, Mina soon married a prominent Boston surgeon, Dr. LeRoi Crandon, in 1918. Crandon, a Mayflower descendant, introduced his vivacious young wife to Boston society. Some of its members thought the new Mrs. Crandon was "too attractive for her own good." Not too concerned, the couple settled into a home at 11 Lime Street on Beacon Hill. Dr. and Mrs. Crandon loved to socialize, and to all outward appearances, seemed an ideal couple. Few knew that Dr. Crandon was a philanderer and his wife had a penchant for alcohol.

When Dr. Crandon read W. J Crawford's book on the Golighter Circle, he shared his new interest with his amused wife. At his suggestion, the couple invited two other couples to their elegant home at 11 Lime Street to try to contact the other side on May 27, 1923. It was more or less a lark, at least on Mina's part. Raps were heard during the séance. In order to discover which of the sitters was the medium, Dr. Crandon asked each one to leave the room. The raps were only heard when his wife Mina was present. Her mediumship took off immediately. She was able to levitate a table in red light, and in a few months she was conducting trumpet séances in her Beacon Hill home. Voices could be heard from as far away as eight feet. The most predominant voice was that of the spirit of her decease brother, Walter, who still spoke in a street-wise manner. As Mina's mediumship became more public, a supporter and editor for *Scientific American,* J. Malcolm Bird, suggested Mina change her name to Margery the Medium to avoid any embarrassment to Dr. Crandon.

Margery Crandon did it all—breezes, raps, trance, writing in several languages, materializations, independent voice, apports, the production of paraffin glove finger prints, and amazing production of ectoplasm. She was even as able to join three solid wood rings in trance, a feat scientifically verified in the United States. Margery Crandon's name should have been synonymous with physical mediumship, just as Houdini's name has come to be one and the same with magic.

However, magic and mediumship are worlds apart. While the magicians are in complete control when they create their tricks, mediums, on the other hand, must be in control of their inner senses to attune to their guides and spirit forces. Magicians are free to utilize misdirection, slight of hand, and flamboyance to create illusions which fool the outer senses. For the most part, magicians are the master of the stage, while mediums attend to two very different worlds, each with its own set of rules. The world of the theatre thrives on excitement—tension is deliberately created to charge the audience. Houdini was known to keep audiences waiting on the edge of their seat for what seemed like hours before he triumphantly emerged from his Chinese Water Torture trick.

However, tension has the opposite effect on mediums. As Reverend Gladys Custance often mentioned in her mediumship circles, "Tension shuts the door." Gladys, by the way, was a professional harpist and hardly shy on stage—unlike most mediums, who are more at home comforting the bereaved. She emphasized also that attitude was important. Doubt and negativity could quickly lower the vibrations of the room. In fact, nothing is more deadly to a séance than skepticism!

Skepticism was definitely in the air when Harry Houdini entered Margery Crandon's séance room on the evening in 1924. His attitude toward Spiritualism, which he summed up in his book, *A Magician Among the Mediums,* was that Spiritualism was a fake. According to Houdini, "nothing more or less than the mental intoxication of words." Houdini was infuriated when he heard that the *Scientific American* was just about to award Margery the prize of $2,500. He asked to be on their investigation team, and then constructed a cabinet with steel bolts and padlocks to secure

Margery during investigation. To her credit Margery submitted to the challenge. Newspaper headlines soon read, "Boston Medium Baffles Experts" followed by "Houdini the Magician Stumped."

No wonder Houdini was stumped, for Margery Crandon's mediumship was extraordinary. Her first feat was to make a bell ring without touching it. With the medium's hands and feet held down by sitters, the bell rang. Next, Walter, the spirit of Margery's brother, moved the megaphone: "A megaphone had been levitating via a spiteful sprite and he (Walter) asked his sister where he should throw it. Houdini asked him to throw the megaphone to him, which appeared to happen, but Houdini had it all figured out."[1]

Houdini went on to claim that Margery had somehow placed the megaphone on her head and simply snapped her head forward to toss the megaphone Houdini's way. If she had pulled off such a ruse, which is most unlikely, Houdini did not explain Walter's voice or independent knowledge. Walter had been quoted as telling the circle earlier, "Houdini's number is up," which proved prophetic when Houdini died three years later.

Houdini was so baffled by Margery's mediumship, that he even stooped to trickery, a ruse which was spotted by Walter. According to psychic researcher, Harry Price, "Margery was immobilized in the wood cabinet, when Walter suddenly shrieked out that Houdini had placed a two foot rule under the cushion on which her feet were resting. The rule was found, but it was never proved whether Houdini had put it there in order to incriminate the medium or if Margery had secreted it so that she could accuse Houdini of trying to ruin her."[2] Calling Houdini "a son of a bitch," Walter accused Houdini of being responsible for the ruler found in Margery's cabinet. Margery protested that she knew nothing of the ruler.

While there was no way to prove or disprove the accusation, the atmosphere of the séance room changed rapidly from cordial to hostile. To Margery Crandon's credit, James Collins, one of Houdini's assistants admitted to planting the ruler many years after the fact. He commented, "I chucked it in the box myself. The boss told me to do it. He wanted to fix her good." However, this news did not come out until 1959, when William Lindsay Gresham published a book which included the following account of that evening.

Houdini's examination of Margery Crandon's mediumship had done its damage. The prize committee consisted of William McDougall, Professor of Psychiatry at Harvard, Harry Houdini, the famous professional conjurer (magician) and escape artist, Walter Franklin Prince, American psychical researcher, Dr. Daniel Fisk Comstock, who introduced Technicolor to film, and Hereward Carrington, amateur conjurer, author, and sponsor for the Italian medium, Eusapia Palladino. Only Carrington voted in favor of Mina after Houdini gave his explanation of what he considered to be "trick mediumship."[3]

Of the group, Hereward Carrington was the most experienced investigator. He gave this report: "As a result of more than forty sittings with Margery, I have arrived at the definite conclusion that genuine supernormal phenomena frequently occur. Many of the observed manifestations might well have been produced fraudulently...however, there remains a number of instances when phenomena were produced and observed under practically perfect control."[3] Not only was there dissent among members of the *Scientific American* committee, but the American Society for Psychical Research was split down the middle—one side for Margery, the other siding with Houdini. The group was so divided, that it disbanded and moved its headquarters to New York.

Undaunted, Margery continued to practice physical mediumship. Later, the American Society of Psychical Research studied Margery Crandson with better results. Her control, her deceased bother, Walter, produced some unusual phenomena: "On certain séances, for example, Walter's voice is reported being heard directly while Margery's mouth was held shut or was filled with liquid or marbles. 'Walter,' so it seems was even able on one occasion to penetrate a sound-proof box so as to activate a microphone which it enclosed, whence his voice was relayed to sitters in another room."[4]

Margery's ability to produce fingerprints on a wax pad also amazed sitters, such as Dr. R. J. Tillyard, who had a private sitting with Margery Crandon on August 10, 1928: It was noted, "During the séance, first of all, thumb marks, whose markings did not resemble the thumb marks of either of the two present, were obtained on various pieces of soft wax, and later in the séance, an independent voice claiming to be the medium's brother, carried on an animated conversation with Dr. Tillyard. That it was independent and apart from the medium, and not her voice was proven by the fact that during the time this voice was speaking, the "Voice Cut Out Machine" was attached to the medium's mouth. This machine is a device which has been invented to make it impossible for the medium, when it is in use, to speak. Therefore, when it is in use, if another voice speaks, it cannot be the medium's."[6]

Another fascinating test conducted in 1928, involved cross correspondence: It all started on March 17th, 1928, when Margery began to write in Chinese, a language that she did not know. Neither she nor the sitters knew Chinese. "Walter announced an experiment in 'cross-correspondence' with Dr. Henry Hardwicke, medium of Niagara Falls, a distance of 450 miles from Boston. He asked Malcolm Bird, then Research Officer of the American Society for Psychical Research, to pick out a sentence which should be given in Chinese through Hardwicke. Malcolm Bird chose: 'A rolling stone gathers no moss.' Hardly was the sitting over when a telegram arrived from Niagara Falls. A few days later it was followed by the original witnessed copy of Dr. Hardwicke's script. It showed a Maltese cross within the circle, a rectangle enclosing the name Kung-fu-tze, the symbols for Bird and Hill, and the Chinese sentence, the general meaning of which is: "A traveling agitator gathers no gold."[7]

Over and over again, Margery proved her mediumship was genuine. Only once did her phenomena fail the laboratory tests. Her credibility came into question when finger prints found on the wax tablet during a later séance turned out to be those of her dentist, who had supplied the soft wax. This is perplexing, since earlier prints had been confirmed as genuine. For example, the prints Walter produced on February 16th, 1932, in the presence of Mr. William H. Button, President of the American Society for Psychical Research, were deemed authentic. One thumb print was even made inside a heavy locked box.[8] Again and again, the finger prints produced by Walter were able to be authenticated by psychic researchers and finger print experts alike.

Walter even astounded the experts by reproducing the thumb prints of an Englishman, Sir Oliver Lodge: "In July, 1931, Walter produced thumb-prints which he declared to be those of Sir Oliver Lodge, who was, at the time, in England, 3,000 miles away. The prints were sent over to England. Mr. Bell, of Scotland Yard, subjected them to a thorough examination and pronounced them identical with the prints of Sir Oliver."[9] The only one piece of evidence, a spirit fingerprint later identified as that of her dentist, was ever found against Margery.

Nevertheless, the public opinion turned against the Crandons when E. E. Dutton announced in 1932, that the Walter's thumb-prints produced in dental wax were found to be identical with those of Margery's dentist. Eileen Garret, a fellow medium who knew Margery well, was quoted as saying, "With her friends, Margery did not need any enemies." Had one of her supposed "friends" switched the wax tablets with the tainted prints? There was certainly ample opportunity, as friends and servants alike were allowed free access to 11 Lime Street.

This doesn't even begin to explain the other fingerprints. In fact, in December of 1933, the American Society for Psychical Research, who studied 300 photographic plates of the finger prints, concluded that:

"1. There is no evidence of fraud, trickery, or the use of any normal mechanism in connection with the séance production of the Walter fingerprint phenomena.
2. These Walter phenomena are definitely proved by the evidence to be supernormal.
3. Neither of the Walter hands as a whole nor as to any of the component parts is identical with that of any known person or persons."[10]

Unfortunately, by then few people cared enough to read their report. For the most part, Margery spent her later years under a cloud of suspicion. In the end, she succumbed to alcoholism after the death of her husband. She carried her secrets to the grave when she passed over in 1941 at the age of fifty-three.

Margery Crandon had lived another fifteen years after her encounter with Harry Houdini. Both died in their fifties, believing that they were right. Margery never gave up her mediumship—even though it hastened her death. Houdini, too, remained steadfast in his beliefs. He published a booklet entitled, *Houdini Exposes the tricks used by the Boston Medium 'Margery*, at his own expense. He became even more famous with his Broadway show, *Houdini*, which featured magic tricks, his famous escapes, and an expose of Spiritualism.

True to Walter's 1924 prediction, "his number was up." While on tour with *Houdini*, the great magician ruptured his appendix when he took a punch to the stomach. Harry Houdini died on his lucky day—October 31, 1926.

Houdini's interest in Spiritualism did not end with the grave. It took another unusual twist with Reverend Arthur Ford, a Spiritualist minister who regarded Houdini as flamboyant and unfair. Reverend Ford, a trance medium, was quite surprised to be told that he had delivered a message from Houdini's mother during a sitting on February 8, 1928. She brought through one word—"forgive"—a word she and her son had chosen as a sign from the other side. According to his friend, Jerome Ellison, Arthur Ford chose not to communicate with the magician's widow; others who were present at the sitting notified Beatrice Houdini that her that her husband had come through with a message.

A séance was arranged for Mrs. Houdini on January 8, 1929. The event which took place in Beatrice Houdini's home included an editor from the *Scientific American* who brought a shorthand expert to take down everything. Jerome Ellison who coauthored Arthur Ford's last book, *The Life Beyond Death* explained, "When the entire code was finished, it was attested by Mrs. Houdini to be in actual fact the long, precisely-worded communication Houdini and his wife had used in their vaudeville act and together agreed upon before Houdini's death as positive identification."[11] What message did Harry Houdini bring through the other side? The letters:

BELIEVE

Sai Baba materializing Vibuthi. Author in lower left.

Glossary

Afterlife
   Life beyond the change called death.

Astral travel
   Condition usually during sleep where the spirit leaves the body and travels into the higher dimensions or other places on earth.

Aura
   Emanations from the spirit body, usually seen as colored lights above the head.

Billet
   Small note or card used in billet séances on which requests or questions for spirit
      are written.

Cabinet
   An enclosed space with a curtain in the front. Here a physical medium sits for the purpose of gathering ectoplasm needed for trumpet and materialization séances.

Chakra
   Sanskit word for wheel. The Hindus believes there are seven etheric energy wheels within the human body.

Circle

A group which forms a circle for the purposes of communicating with spirit.

Clairaudience

The ability to hear spirit voices with the inner ear or fifth chakra.

Clairgustance

The ability to taste and smell spirit through the inner senses.

Clairsentience

The ability to sense spirit usually through the solar plexus or third chakra.

Clairvoyance

The ability to see spirit with the third eye or sixth chakra.

Ectoplasm

A cloudy substance which is extruded through orifices of the medium and the solar plexus for the purpose of physical manifestation of spirit.

Electronic Voice Phenomena (EVP)

The recorded sounds of spirit voices and activity.

Gate-keeper

A particular spirit guide who stands at the threshold between the two words to protect the entranced medium. The gate-keeper acts as a master of ceremony for the other spirit who wishes to come through the medium.

Guides

Spirits of deceased loved ones, advanced teachers, and sometimes angels who offer their encouragement and assistance.

Inspirational writing

Information which is given directly through spirit through the inner faculties, especially the heart or fourth chakra.

Laying on of hands

Method of healing in which the healer places his or her hands, usually over head, shoulders, and heart of the individual seeking healing.

Materialization

This occurs when spirit appears during a séance or other circumstance. During a materialization spirit can be seen with with the outer eye.

Meditation

A relaxed state in which one goes inward for development, healing, or guidance.

Medium

A person who is sensitive to the vibrations from the other side of life and therefore able to communicate with the other side.

Mental mediumship

Use of the inner senses of clairsentience, clairaudience, and clairvoyance to communicate with the other side.

Orbs

Circular white lights which indicate spirit presence. Sometimes Spirit faces or other details are seen in the center of the orb.

Percipitated pictures

A rare form of mediumship in which images that are literally impressed or precipitated onto cards and canvass by spirit.

Physical mediumship

Mediumship in which some form of physical phenomena is produced that can be detected by the outer senses.

Psychic

A person who intuits information. A psychic is not necessarily receiving information from spirit.

Psychic photography

Photographs of orbs, mists, spirit shadows, or even full figures and faces of deceased persons.

Psychic surgery

A rare form of medical mediumship in which the spirit doctor actually performs a form of surgery. Unlike regular surgery, there is little if any pain.

Reading

A session with a medium or psychic for the purposes of receiving information through super-normal channels. In England, the term used is a sitting.

Séance

French word for sitting. Here people gather in a darkened room for the purposes of communicating with spirit.

Spirit art

Images or portraits produced by a medium though a spirit guide or the use of clairvoyance.

Spirit cards

Cards, usually three-by-five index cards, on which spirit draws or precipitates pictures and names of spirits.

Spiritualism

The science, religion, and philosophy that believes in life after death and the ability to communicate with sprit.

Synchronicity

Events that are coincidental in nature.

Table-tipping

The ability to move or tip a table by psychokinesis (PK) or spirit energy.

Trance

A deeply relaxed state of mediumship which can range from a light state of induction to full or "dead" trance.

Trumpet

The cone usually made of aluminum approximately three feet high used in trumpet séances.

Endnotes

Introduction

1. Carolyn Cassady, *Off the Road*, Penguin Books, New York, NY, page 277.

Chapter One

1. Jon Klimo, *Channeling*, North Atlantic Book, Berkeley CA, 1998, page 106.

2. Jon Klimo, *Channeling*, North Atlantic Book, Berkeley CA, 1998, page 106.

3. Jon Klimo, *Channeling*, North Atlantic Book, Berkeley CA, 1998, page 107

4. Dr. Jeffery Mislove, *Roots of Consciousness*, Council Oak Books, Tulsa OK, 1993, pages 37-38.

5. Dr. Jeffery Mislove, *Roots of Consciousness*, Council Oak Books, Tulsa OK, 1993, page 38.

6. Dr. Jeffery Mislove, *Roots of Consciousness*, Council Oak Books, Tulsa OK, 1993, page 38-39.

7. Dr. Jeffery Mislove, *Roots of Consciousness*, Council Oak Books, Tulsa OK, 1993, pages 39-40.

8. Dr. Jeffery Mislow, *Roots of Consciousness*, Council Oak Books, Tulsa OK, 1993, page 44.

9. Ascended Masters: http://www.tsl.org/ascendedmasters/, page 1.

Chapter Two

1. Raymond Buckland, *Buckland's Book of Spirit Communication*, Llewellyn Worldwide Publications, St. Paul MN, 2004, page 28.

2. Raymond Buckland, *Buckland's Book of Spirit Communication*, Llewellyn Worldwide Publications, St. Paul MN, 2004, page 28.

3. Raymond Buckland, *Buckland' Book of Spirit Communication*, Llewellyn Worldwide Publications, St. Paul MN, 2004, page 30.

4. Harriet M. Shelton, *Abraham Lincoln Returns*, page 182.

5. Francine Hornberger *The World's Greatest Psychics*, Citadel Press, New York, NY, page 171.

Chapter Three

1. A. Gauld, *The Founders of Psychical Research*, London: Routledge and Kegan, Paul, 1968, page 69.

2. Rosemary Guiley, *Harper's Encyclopedia of Mystical Paranormal Experience*, Harper Collins, New York, NY, page 26.

3. N. Riley Heagery, "The Mediumship of the Eddy Brothers," http// Noah Arc Society.com, 2002.

4. N. Riley Heagery, "The Mediumship of the Eddy Brothers", Http// Noah Arc Society.com, 2002.

5. N. Riley Heagery, "The Mediumship of the Eddy Brothers" Http//Noah's Arc Society. com, 2002.

6. N. Riley Heagerty, *The French Revelation*, Morris Publishing, Kearney, NE, page 311.

7. Francine Hornberger, *The World's Greatest Psychics*, Citadel Press, 2004, New York, NY page 171.

8. Estelle Roberts, *Fifty Years A Medium*, Herbert Jenkins, London, 1959, page 100-103.

9. Harry Edwards, *The Mediumship of Jack Weber*, Anchor Press Ltd, 1974, pages 84. and 85.

10. Sidney Kirkpatrick, *Edgar Cayce: An American Prophet*, Penguin, Putnam, Inc., New York, 2000, page 459.

11. Sidney Kirkpatrick, *Edgar Cayce: An American Prophet*, Penguin, Putnam, Inc., New York, 2000, page 465.

12. Iving Litvag, *Singer in the Shadow*, McMillan Company, New York, 1972, page 207.

13. Elwood Babbitt and Charles Hapgood, *The God Within*, Fine Line Books, Turners Falls, MA, 1982, page 80.

14. Elwood Babbitt and Charles Hapgood, *The God Within*, Fine Line Books, Turners Falls, MA, 1982, page 303.

Chapter Four

1. *Tibetan Book of Mental Development,* Dharmsala University, India.

2. *Tibetan Book of Mental Development,* Dharmsala University, India page 154.

3. *Tibetan Book of Mental Development,* Dharmsala University, India page 158.

Chapter Five

1. *The Perfect Medium,* Yale University Press, New Haven, CT 2005, page 21.

2. Fred Gettings, *Ghosts in Photograph*, Optimum Publishing Co, 1978, page 23.

3. Fred Gettings, *Ghosts in Photograph*, Optimum Publishing Co, 1978, page 25.

4. Photography Museum: http://www.photography-museum.com.

5. Fred Gettings, *Ghosts in Photograph*, Optimum Publishing Co, 1978, page 25.

6. *Return to the Haunted Museum Section of the Website,* Copyright 2003 by Troy Taylor. All Rights Reserved.

7. Return to the Haunted Museum Section of the Website, Copyright 2003 by Troy Taylor. All Rights Reserved.

8. Fred Gettings, *Ghosts in Photograph,* Optimum Publishing Co., 1978, page 28.

9. Prairie Ghosts: http://www.prairieghosts.com/hope.html.

10. Fred Gettings, *Ghosts in Photograph,* Optimum Publishing Co., 1978.

11. The Ghost Research Society, headquartered in Oaklawn, Illinois.

12. Enid Hoffman, *Develop Your Psychic Skills,* Whitford Press, PA, page 117.

13. Grant and Jane Solomon, *The Scole Experiment,* London, England, Judy Piatkus Publishers, 2003, page xi.

14. Grant and Jane Solomon, *The Scole Experiment,* London, England, Judy Piatkus Publishers, 2003, page 57.

Chapter Six

1. Tom and Lisa Butler, *There is No Death and There Are No Dead*, Reno, NV: AA-EVP Publishing, 2004, page 44.

2. Tom and Lisa Butler, *There is No Death and There Are No Dead*, Reno, NV: AA-EVP Publishing, 2004, page 7.

3. Tom and Lisa Butler, *There is No Death and There Are No Dead*, Reno, NV: AA-EVP Publishing, 2004, page 8.

4. Jeff Balanger, *Communicating With the Dead,* Franklin Lakes, NJ: New Page Books, 2001, page 115.

5. Mary Roach, *Spook: Science Tackles the Afterlife,* New York NY: W. W. Norton and Company 2005, pages 183-184.

6. Tom and Lisa Butler, *There is No Death and There Are No Dead,* Reno, NV: AA-EVP Publishing, 2004, page 120.

7. Tom and Lisa Butler, *There is No Death and There Are No Dead,* Reno, NV: AA-EVP Publishing, 2004, page 163.

8. Tom and Lisa Butler, *There is No Death and There Are No Dead,* Reno, NV: AA-EVP Publishing, 2004, page 33.

9. Tom and Lisa Butler, *There is No Death and There Are No Dead,* Reno, NV: AA-EVP Publishing, 2004, page 22.

11. Tom and Lisa Butler, *There is No Death and There Are No Dead,* Reno, NV: AA-EVP Publishing, 2004, page 9.

12. Tom and Lisa Butler, *There is No Death and There Are No Dead,* Reno, NV: AA-EVP Publishing, 2004, page 29.

13. Tom and Lisa Butler, *There is No Death and There Are No Dead,* Reno, NV: AA-EVP Publishing, 2004, page 29.

14. Grant and Jane Solomon, *The Scole Experiment*, London, England, Judy Piatkus Publishers, 2003, page 113.

15. Grant and Jane Solomon, *The Scole Experiment,* London, England, Judy Piatkus Publishers, 2003, page 24.

16. Grant and Jane Solomon, *The Scole Experiment,* London, England, Judy Piatkus Publishers, 2003, pages 24-25.

17. American Association of Electronic Voice Phenomena: http://www.aaevp.com/.

Chapter Seven

1. Dr. Douglas Baker, *Opening the Third Eye*, Hertfordshire, England: Little Elephant Press, 1993, page 80.

2. Love Without End: http://www.lightparty.com/Spirituality/Love-WithoutEnd.html.

3. Edgar Cayce reading 5355-1.

4. Edgar Cayce reading 5355-1.

5. Alice Bailey, *Discipleship in the New Age, Volume II*, New York, NY: Lucius Publishing Company, page 7.

6. *The Tibetan Book of Mental Development*, Dharmsala University, India, page 154.

7. *The Tibetan Book of Mental Development*, Dharmsala University, India.

Chapter Eight

1. Klilmo, *Channeling*, North Atlantic Books, Berkely, CA 1987, page 1.

Chapter Nine

1. Charles H. Hapgood, *Talks with Christ*, Fine Line Books, 1981, Turners Falls, MA, page 139.

2. Charles H. Hapgood, *Talks with Christ*, Fine Line Books, 1981, Turners Falls, MA, page 201.

3. Paul Solomon, http://www.facim.org/acim/description.htm.

4. Paul Solomon, http://www.paulsolomon.com/page5.html.

5. A Course in Miracleshttp://www.paulsolomon.com/page5. html.

6. W. Alexander Wheeler, *The Prophetic Revelations of Paul Solomon, Sam Weiser*, 1994, York Beach ME, pages 165-166.

7. Paul Solomon: http://www.paulsolomon.com/page5.html.

8. Paul Solomon: http://www.paulsolomon.com/page5.html.

9. Gordon Michael Scallion, *Notes From the Cosmos*, Matrix Institute, 1997, West Chesterfield, NH, page 289.

10. Crystal Links: http://www.crystalinks.com/gordon.html.

11. Crystal Links: http://www.marysnewsletter.com/spiritlk.htm.

12. Ronna Herman: http://www.ronnastar.com/starquest4.

Chapter Ten

1. Spirit: http://www.lifepositive.com/Spirit/new-age-path/spiritual-healing/psychicsurgery.asp.

2. http://freespace.virgin.net/russel.steward/healpeep.htm.

3. Thomas Sugrue, *There Is A River*, Reading 1928.

4. John G. Fuller, *Arigo: Surgeon of the Rusty Knife*, Pocket Books, 1974, New York, NY, page 21.

5. Psychic Adventures: http://groups.msn.com/PsychicAdventuresOnline/ famouspsychics.msnw.

6. Psychic Adventures: http://groups.msn.com/PsychicAdventuresOnline/famouspsychics.msnw.

7. Spirit: http://www.lifepositive.com/Spirit/new-age-path/spiritual healing/psychicsurgery.asp.

8. Prime Time: http://abcnews.go.com/Health/Primetime/story?id.

Chapter Eleven

None

Chapter Twelve

1. Tom Johanson: www.Tomjohanson.com.

2. Tom Johanson: www.Tomjohanson.com.

3. Coral Polge: http://website.lineone.net/~enlightenment/coral_polge.htm.

4. Source: "The Bangs Sisters and their Precipitated Spirit Portraits," Publisher/Date Unknown.

5. Compiled by Irene Swann, Helt Memorial Art Gallery, Chesterfield, IN, 1969.

6. Ron Nagy, *Precipitated Spirit Paintings*, 2006, Glade Press, Inc., Lakeville, MN, page 59.

7. Ron Nagy, *Precipitated Spirit Paintings*, 2006, Glade Press, Inc., Lakeville, MN, page 59.

8. Ron Nagy, *Precipitated Spirit Paintings,* 2006, Glade Press, Inc., Lakeville, MN, page 63.

9. Ron Nagy, *Precipitated Spirit Paintings,* 2006, Glade Press, Inc., Lakeville, MN pages 63-67.

10. Ron Nagy, *Precipitated Spirit Paintings*, 2006, Glade Press, Inc., Lakeville, MN, page 68.

11. Ron Nagy, *Precipitated Spirit Paintings*, 2006, Glade Press, Inc., Lakeville, MN, page 69.

Chapter Thirteen

1. Buckland, Raymond, *Buckland's Book of Spirit Communications*, Llewellyn Worldwide, St. Paul MN, 2004, page 152.

2. Fodor, Nandor, Encyclopedia of Psychic Sciences, University Books, New York, NY, 1966.

3. Fodor, Nandor, Encyclopedia of Psychic Sciences, University Books, New York, NY, 1966.

4. Jefts, Lena Barnes, *A Treatise on Physical Mediumship,* Camp Silver Belle booklet.

5. Jinarajadasa, C., *Letters from the Masters of Wisdom,* Theosophical Publishing House, Madras, India, 1977, page 33.

6. Jefts, Lena Barnes, *Lo I Am With You Always*, Distributed by the National Assocation of Spiritualist Churcxhes, Lily Dale, NY, pages 28 and 29.

7. Source: http://www.prairieghosts.com/florence.html.

8. Fodor, Nandor, *An Encyclopaedia of Psychic Science*, University Books, New York, NY, 1934.

9. N. Riley Heagery "The Mediumship of the Eddy Brothers," Http//www.The Noah Arc Society, 2002.

10. Helen Dunscan: http://www.helenduncan.org.uk.

11. Jefts, Lena Barnes, *A Treatise on Physical Mediumship*, Camp Silver Belle booklet.

12. Jefts, Lena Barnes, *A Treatise on Physical Mediumship*, Camp Silver Belle booklet.

13. Jefts, Lena Barnes, *Lo I am With You Always*, Camp Silver Belle booklet, page 37.

14. Jefts, Lena Barnes, *Lo I am With You Always*, Camp Silver Belle booklet, page 39.

15. Grant and Jane Solomon, *The Scole Experiment*, London, England, Judy Piatkus Publishers, 2003, pages 65-66.

16. Grant and Jane Solomon, *The Scole Experiment*, London, England, Judy Piatkus Publishers, 2003, page 11.

17. Kubler-Ross, Elisabeth, *The Wheel of Life*, New York, NY, 1997, page 177.

18. Kubler-Ross, Elisabeth, *The Wheel of Life*, New York, NY, 1997, page 177.

Chapter Fourteen

1. Francine Hornberger, *The World's Greatest Psyhics*, Citadel Books, 2004, New York, NY, page 170.

2. Harry Price, *Fifty Years of Psychical Research*, Longman, Gren, and Company, London England, 1939, page 112.

3. Mina Crandon: http://en.wikipedia.Org/wik/Mina-Crandon.

4. Margery Crandon: Htttp://www.fst/org/Margery.htm.

5. John Beloff, *Parapsychology:A Concise History*, St. Martin;s Press, New York, NY, 1993, page 110.

6. Arthur Findlay, *On the Edge of the Etheric*, Spritualist National Union Publications, 1951, London, England, page 30.

7. Survival After Death: http://www.survivalafterdeath.org/books/fodor/chapter 23htm.

8. Survival After Death: http://wwwsurivalafterdeath.org/books/fodor/chapter 23htm.

9. Survival After Death: http://wwwsurivalafterdeath.org/books/fodor/chapter 23htm.

10. Survival After Death: http://wwwsurivalafterdeath.org/books/fodor/chapter 23htm.

11. Arthur Ford and Jerome Ellison, *The Life Beyond Death*, G.Pl Putnam and Sons, New York, NY, 1971, page 17.

Index